YOU ARE GOING TO MAKE IT!
Walking Through Emotions
This Too Shall Pass

BY

LUCILLE D. ANKUM

DEDICATION

Dear Precious Women of God,
this book was written especially for you.
I promise that something better is waiting for you!

TABLE OF CONTENTS

PREFACE

I wanted to write about real life, real experiences, true journeys and raw emotions — the feelings of everyday living amidst the trauma and drama of divorce.

It's true that women often find themselves being put on the back burner, especially after a divorce. The fact is, no one knows what to do with us. The world quickly labels us as this or that, and I should know. I had to carry on after a divorce, and it meant dealing with that awful period of time after everything finalized. In that post-mortem moment there is no turning back, and instead we must "turn the page" and begin a new chapter. No one can tell your story like you, and within these pages I share mine.

Some have no idea what others go through during or after a divorce. Being Christians, we are told we should be able to handle anything — and it's true that we can get through with the help of God. But we also need the support of others to help us grow and heal and move on. It can be difficult as others judge or cast stones. Why do Believers behave so cruelly, when Jesus has commanded us to show compassion?

At times I have noticed that some Christians seem to "smell weakness" or "smell blood" when some poor, unfortunate person is facing a divorce. Why are they so quick to "eat their wounded?" Is this a proper Christian response to someone's suffering — to kick people when they are down? Of course not. How quickly their perspectives change when the shoe is on the other foot. How humbling it is to be on the receiving end of those slings and arrows. This book is written to share the experiences women go through before, during and after divorce. It is meant to illuminate and change the hearts of those who should be supporting fellow Christians in a time of need.

We are called to help each other, and especially help women who are facing personal devastation. May this resource bless you and help you cope, bloom and overcome as you finish the mission God has ordained for you. You are loved, you are blessed, and YOU ARE GOING TO MAKE IT!

ACKNOWLEDGMENTS

Throughout my life's journey many people have earned my thanks, especially my children and grandchildren. To my daughter Justina and my son Clint (along with my nine wonderful grandchildren), I thank God for you. You are my heroes, and without your Godly obedience and advice it would have been very difficult to complete this book.

INTRODUCTION
PUTTING MY LIFE IN ORDER

How do we make order out or chaos? In putting my life in order, I began with God first. The word of God in Matthew 6:33 is a great place to start: "Seek ye first the kingdom of God, and His Righteousness, and all these things shall be added unto you."

The first time I got saved, I stayed saved, because there was never any need to go back. All I knew and wanted was God. I searched for years trying to find Him, until one night in 1994 when I dreamed a dream that would change my life forever. I recall that troubled slumber so vividly. In my dream the world was ending… and I was on my way to hell. Then I heard a still, soft voice say, "I am going to give you one more chance."

The following Sunday I visited a church for the second time. When the pastor gave the altar call, guess what? You guessed it! I was the first person to stand. As I nervously walked forward I bowed my head and lifted my hands, and when it came my turn… it happened! After repeating a few words, I suddenly became a born again Christian. The pastor continued to stand in front of me, and looked at me as he said these words:

"God is going to use you."

He was right, and that is exactly what happened. And God is still using me as I share a part of my life to bless yours. Yes, divorce is seldom pleasant. It comes with its fair share of heartache and a dose of defeat. But my mission is to let you know there is nothing too hard for God. I would like to share the same life-changing prayer I prayed that Sunday.

Lord God,

I know that I am a sinner, and your word says if I confess with my mouth the Lord Jesus and believe in my heart that God raised Jesus from the dead that I too am saved. I believe you died for my sins and rose again. I turn from sin and invite you to come into my heart and live. I except and follow you as my Lord and Savior in Jesus' name. -- Roman 10:9-10

YOU ARE BLESSED.

CHAPTER ONE

A SPECIAL MOMENT

In Memory of Edgar Ankum (1913-1999), I dedicate this chapter to my Daddy. Thank you for teaching me that it is okay to cry.

Never Too Old to Cry:

My Dad was 87 years old when he passed away. At times, especially later in life, he would become emotional. Yet as a young man he never cried in front of others, for it was definitely considered wrong. He was taught, and later taught us, that tears are a sign of weakness.

Thankfully, with age comes wisdom. Eventually, Daddy allowed himself to weep in front of us. Once he got started, there was no stopping him. He kept on until he got it all out. Witnessing this, I slowly realized there is something both noble and cathartic about a man (or woman) shedding tears. Those special occasions when Daddy showed his vulnerable side will always stay with me. It taught me that tears are nature's balm. They are healing drops. And I thank my father for teaching me this life-changing lesson, for my own tears have been my writing fuel.

I LOVE YOU, DADDY.

IT'S OKAY TO CRY

I cannot count the numerous times I have started writing this book, but stopped after the first chapter. I said to myself, "I am going to do it this time, for sure!" Certainly, I have experienced enough adventures throughout my lifetime to write many books... and if I could only get beyond the first chapter I knew I would finally finish what I started.

Growing up I never cried much. Like my father in his formative years, I believed that crying was a sign of weakness. In other words, you were not handling yourself very well if you cried. Of course, this philosophy changed over the years as we watched Daddy benefit from crying. Thank heavens I followed suit, because writing is an emotional journey. Tears, you see, are the keys to unlocking the narrative.

I had a lot of crying to do in order to get this book published. Like Daddy, once I started bawling I couldn't stop. It seemed like anything and everything would trigger the floodgates. At first, I honestly thought something was wrong with me. After all, crying was such an unfamiliar response and I wasn't exactly comfortable with the onslaught of visible emotion. In years past, if I got sad around my children I would go in to the next room and cry, or just play it off. I didn't want them to see any kind of weakness in me. Now, even watching cartoons with my grandchildren can bring tears, especially if there is a sad ending.

What a great relief it has been to let it all out (and still be considered normal). In hindsight, I fought so hard to maintain an image of sanity, and since crying was an image of insanity, I didn't want anyone to think I was crazy. Now, the personal therapy of writing and the weeping has unbound everything I've internalized over the decades. In fact, writing this book has given me the chance to express myself in ways I could never imagine.

So I wrote this book for my loved ones and others who have been conditioned to repress their tears. Guess what? IT'S OKAY

TO CRY!

The bottom line is that crying is good for you. Letting it all out is quite freeing. Did bottling up my emotions over the years help one bit? No. So one day I just let it all go and I have been crying ever since! Honestly, when you cry you are shedding more than tears. My body felt as though it was going through a filtering process and flushing away all the hurt. The pain was replaced with healing.

Tears are an emotional salve, and I couldn't complete my manuscript without them. But when you aren't quite ready to face a painful past, you can struggle with emotional gridlock. This is why I froze when writing the first chapter! Somehow I thought the writer's block would go away, but it didn't. It took a watershed of tears to clear my mind and prepare me to tackle one of the most important projects of my life.

Each effort to write was a "start and stop" exercise and reminded me of giving birth. Picture this: You've become pregnant and have carried the baby for nine months. At last you are in position to give birth, but all the sudden your brain says, "I've changed my mind! This pain is too much!" Well, babies (and books) simply must be born, no matter how excruciating the process. It's a matter of staying on the birthing table, bearing down, and achieving something wonderful.

I still recall the first moments after my first child was born. By staying focused and "pushing through," I was rewarded. I was able to hold the fruits of my labor in my arms — my very own baby girl. As she snuggled against me for the first time, I knew the labor was worth it. I had ushered a new life into the world. God had a mission for my child, as He does for all his children. And I believe my book (which I also call my baby) also has a mission. My hope is that people will be helped in so many ways, because I stayed in position and birthed a memoir written by a divorced woman, for divorced women.

You see, it's not about me. It's about you. Funny how endeavoring on behalf of other people brings multiple blessings. As you tackle your own destiny, don't let emotional constipation, labor pains or anything else stop you from doing your own thing. Your mission is to step out, and who knows what lives you will impact?

Go ahead and cry yourself into victory. And while you are at it, know that you are going to make it.

Soon I completed the first chapter of my memoir and found myself at the beginning of the next chapter. I cried even more, but this time not out of frustration. Now I experienced tears of joy. My writing and weeping had gone to another level, and I finally discovered the road I was to travel. I could now write about something that had bound and kept me tied up for years.

I used to be very afraid to let it all out and share the truth of all my ups and downs. Showing no emotion at all seemed one way to spare everyone's feelings. People thought I was strong because I didn't look defeated or worried. Boy, were they mistaken! Again, it relates back to my first birthing experience. My labor pains were so intense that I became numb. The doctor took one look at me and automatically assumed that I wasn't ready to deliver. His exact words were, "I don't think she is ready yet, because she is not looking ugly enough."

Even at my mother's home going I had a cousin ask me why I wasn't crying. She said, "Honey, you must be strong." How easy for people to misinterpret emotions. My ability to hide my emotions was often mistaken for emotional strength. People may think you have it all together... when, in reality, you are crumbling inside.

In my case I had nothing together, especially at home. At home I was a mess! There were times in my marriage when my husband and I both said some terrible words. The more I stayed in church I realized how powerful words could be, so I did my best to stay away from zingers, word bombs and alphabet missiles. Yet often I was on the receiving end. I would hear my husband say to me, "You will never be anything but a door mat," and all I could do was cry. I was not a violent person and would not have dared raise my hand. I just took those insults and stored them all in a place in my heart.

You will have seasons when all you do is cry and you won't know why. I try to keep a box of tissue by my bed along with paper and pencil. I believe all our tears mean something to God, and I want to be ready in case He wants to speak to me.

So go ahead — it's okay to cry!

Remember my comparison to the book verses childbirth? Well, the truth is, we are created for something to come out of us, whether it be a book or not. What inspirations you choose becomes the father of what is developed in you, so pick wisely.

God's child eyes are shiny and bright,
God's child heart is clean and true.
God's child hands are gentle and smooth,
God's child smile is genuine and not blue.
This is God's handy work — how perfect.
He puts us together by His hand and not glue.

LET GO AND LET GOD

MANY times I have heard people say, "Just let go and let God." Do you suppose they know what this means, or are just saying it because it sounds deep? For some, living up to this cliché is easier said than done, especially when they have been in a relationship for a long period of time. We cannot expect people to "let go" of the ingrained love, history, slights and injustices they have experienced, no matter how "deep" or intellectual they may seem.

When it comes to divorce, I think at times this statement can do more harm than good. For example, when someone hears "You need to let go," but are unable to let go, they may question themselves. They may doubt themselves and ask internally, "What's wrong with me?" They are still processing the good and bad times they had with their loved one and end up feeling worse.

In my case, the words stung deeply because I was not over "him" yet. It seems as though I could not win, so that was the last thing I need to hear right then. Although, the letting go came with time, it was something I had to experience on my own clock and at my own pace. For women, especially, there needs to be the flexibility and opportunity to mourn. Then they can let their man go and know they will be okay.

It takes work to keep a relationship going, and it takes work to move on. Be mindful as you let go of your mate that you must not let go of God. You might not need your mate anymore, but you will surely need God on this new journey you are about to experience.

That's why the phrase "Let go and let God," can be so trite. Yes, we can "let go" and we can "let God," but it is a process — an emotional release combined with a leap of faith. Some of us are so caught up in anxiety, grief and turmoil that we miss God's message: "Let go. Let go, I got it." Instead we hold on to our old hurts and pain. We block out the "good voice" in favor of the bad voice that says, "I cannot let go yet." I, personally, am no different than you. I am guilty of listening to the taunt inside my head that said, "There is no way I can go on without this man in my life."

What did I do to reclaim my life? I sought out a Christian counselor. My counselor taught me an exercise that I want to share with you.

My Steps to Freedom:

- Cut out about 20 small pieces of paper.

- Write down on each sheet all the hurt and pain you are feeling.

- Put each sheet in order according to the pain.

- Study sheet one. Look at it and take your time. Ask yourself are you willing to let go or hold onto it a while. It is okay if you are not ready to let go right now, and if that's the case simply put it aside and move to the next.

- Work through the stack. If you are ready and willing to let go of an issue, look at it for one last time, then tear it up and throw it away.

God healed me as I slowly began to throw each sheet away. Near the end I had two sheets left, only because I was not ready to let go yet. Yet after hearing my counselor say one last time, "It is time to let go," I finally tore up those sheets and loosed the chains once and for all. I left it all behind, every hurt and pain that

I had been carrying around. I started to live again and began to enjoy a life free of constant reminders of what had happened during my past relationship.

What I am sharing is real. God wants to heal all of you and wants you to leave no sheets behind. If you can let go, God has guaranteed to fill that empty spot with Himself. Not that there won't be challenges... there will! In my case, after one month had passed I was doing well, until all the sudden a flood of worry seemed to overwhelm me. Thank God, the timing was perfect. I could not wait to tell my counselor about the panic attacks.

Before I could get it out of my mouth, it was as if he knew what I was going to say. He sat me down in a chair in front of him (as he always did) and looked straight at me. Then he said, "Let me tell you this before we get started. None of this is going to be easy for you right now. You are at a crossroad in your life. You have some great challenges ahead, and the first battle will start in your mind."

There was something about him that got my attention. I would always look straight into my counselor's eyes and know this man was good. He knew how to counsel me in a way that I could receive it. I knew God had sent him into my life to help me move on, so I paid close attention to whatever he had to tell me and followed it to the tee.

Of course, he wanted my feedback. "Let me tell you what happen to me," I told him. "All of a sudden I started to worry and could not stop."

Then he said to me, "I have another exercise I want you to try." He told me to put a large rubber band loosely around my wrist, and every time a negative thought came in my mind I was to pop it. Then I was to say out loud, "STOP! I will think on good things according to Phil 4-8: 'For the rest brethren, whatever is true, whatever is worthy of reverence and is honorable and seemly, whatever just, whatever is pure, whatever is lovable, whatever is kind and winsome and gracious, if there is any virtue and excellence, if there is anything worthy of phrase, think on and weigh and take account of these things.'"

I was to wear the rubber band for two weeks and keep notes on a little red index card. God has all kinds of ways to help you. He knows the right people to propel into your life at a certain time. He can cause others to speak the precise words you need to hear. And after two weeks my arm was sore from snapping the bands, but it worked. It also reminded me that God feels what you and I feel. He wants to see us delivered and free from whatever bondage we are carrying.

Just look at it this way. Ask yourself if you are willing to forgive this person, even if they never said "I am sorry." The moment you let go, God starts to heal you. That is how awesome He is. It is not an easy thing to endure, especially if you have a broken heart. But just think how your divorce must have broken God's heart, for a marriage is a covenant agreement that is joined together by God Himself. Now it is broken, yet God's love is bigger than a break up. His love is deeper than our own sins, frailties, pride and neediness. His love is everything we need to move forward and be what he has called us to be.

Once the light bulb went on, I stopped focusing on myself. It is selfish to only think about how a divorce is affecting you, especially when there are other people involved. One thing to remember is that even though your husband is gone and your marriage is broken, you still have God. He will never leave you and has promised to stick to you closer than a brother. So run to Him. He is waiting just for you.

A PRAYER OF LETTING GO:

Dear God please help me to let go of (finish in your own words).

TRUSTING GOD

In this section I want to remind you of four things, and I'm making it plain and simple:

- Do not worry

- Do not fret

- Do not be afraid

- Trust God completely

If these are the only things you get out of this book, then you have done well.

How do you trust God? If you don't know how, here's a simple primer.

- Get rid of doubt

- Get rid of unbelief

- Get rid of frustration

- Believe God

Everything you need is in the Bible. Do not ever replace the Bible for any book — not this one or any other. This memoir is meant to encourage you as you go through some difficult times.

But it will never, ever replace the Bible, which is God's final word and covers every circumstance and situation you will ever encounter. The holy word is your instruction manual, so please do not neglect it.

In fact, you should read your Bible first, and then ask God to give you understanding. You are about to go through a lot of "stuff" which will help prepare you for your new life. We are all books waiting to be written, so think of this next year as a 365-page manuscript just waiting to be filled. Every day will bring some blessing, if only we can recognize it! We all have a mission, and if God can use me, He can surely use you. So go ahead and do what God is calling you to do. It is already inside of you waiting to be born.

After your divorce, your life does not have to end. It's a great time to be alive, so live your life to the fullest and see what God has in store for you. Start enjoying where you are, even after you have a bad day with the lawyer. One day after my appointment with my divorce attorney, I left that office feeling the worst ever. I remember it being a very hot day, so I stopped by the grocery store. There I saw the best-looking watermelons I had ever seen. I knew I only had two one-dollar bills and the watermelons were $5.00. Yet as I reached in my purse, suddenly three more one dollar bills and some change just appeared. It was enough to purchase the watermelon. When I got home and prepared my tasty treat, I heard this soft voice in my spirit say, "ENJOY."

What I am saying to you is simple. You need to take little breaks. In the midst of lawyers and kids and bills... take a break. No matter what season it is, go buy a watermelon. After having my day end so beautifully, the devil (a liar) tried to steal my joy. I received an e-mail from my ex-husband's lawyer stating I lost my house. In fact I ended up owing him money, plus it got worse. A lien was placed against me. I was afraid and intimidated because I did not know much about liens, other than it was not something to be taken lightly.

I kept hearing a taunting whisper in my ear all night: "You are going to jail if you do not pay that money back now!" Oh, the devil was having fun torturing me, and I tossed all through the wee hours trying to think of how to get out of this mess. At that moment I could not do any of the things my counselor taught me to do. Fear had me paralyzed.

How did I break free from the fear? I had to repent first for letting worry take hold of me. I knew God's word enough to know better, but I missed it that time. There will be times when we all miss it. Do not take it so hard that you can't get back up again, for that is exactly what I was determined to do. I got back up. God made it simple for me. Again I heard in my spirit, "Do not worry, do not fret, and trust God."

Fear can damage you in such a way that it can be difficult to recover. Remember, the devil is a master manipulator and loves nothing more than to kick you when you are down, or trip you up when you are unsteady. Certainly, there was no reason for me not to have gone crazy other than God. Now as I look back, I know God kept me sane for a reason. He meant for me to write this book and tell you that you are going to make it, too! God is the same and does not change. We can count on Him — and we can all thank Him for that.

I had to title this book according to what I kept hearing: "You are going to make it." Yes, we are all going to make it. Only God knows how — I certainly had no idea! But God knows the outcome beforehand, and that is why we can trust Him. He is like a traffic monitor that can see an accident up ahead. The devil cannot do that. The devil also knows you are somebody and is hoping that you don't discover how powerful you really are... and who you are as a child of God. If that evil creature can plant seeds of fear and unbelief in your head, he has you.

You see, God's hands are tied when you fail to stand on his promises. But you can avoid that trap and become an overcomer by claiming the promises in God's word. Say with your mouth and believe in your heart that you are going to trust God no matter what.

If you are being tempted by worry, please continue to STAND and believe God's word. God won't be mocked, and He wasn't joking in Proverb 3:5-6: Trust in the Lord with all thine heart, and lean not unto thine own understanding, in all thy ways acknowledge Him and he shall direct they path.

I had no other choice but to trust God. Who else could get me out of the mess my life had become? The enemy does not play fair. If it was not for the Lord, what would most of us do? In my particular situation, my mother and father had passed away. Being from a family of 10 children, it seemed I should have had someone on my side who understood what I was going through. However, you may find at times you stand alone... and all you have is God. That is when you will know you are in His hands and nothing can separate His love from you.

When you start to develop this kind of love and confidence for God, the next thing you know, you are on your way to trusting Him. And that is ALWAYS better than trusting solely in a man. Yet how many of us have replaced God with a man? We let a special male take us out and spend money on us. Right away, we introduce him to our kids, move him in the next day, stake a claim, and think he is the one sent to us from God. In our minds, we feel we had no other choice and try to justify our actions. How else were we going to make ends meet? Our little job was never going to be enough to provide for our families. And our biological clocks are ticking... so we need a man!

Time and again women are prone to fall into this trap. If this describes you, just know that you are not alone. And what is the lesson? It is wiser to trust the maker of men, the creator of the universe! Men are fallible, but God is infallible. This became obvious during the fallout of my marriage and the difficulties of my divorce. Thank God for Psalm 37, which I read over and over again. This is what God gave me to stand on and it kept me sane.

I am no different than you. I am a fallible woman, and God allowed me to go through some extreme circumstances during my marriage. I had my mind made up that I was not giving up without a fight, and that was exactly what I had on my hands. In the spirit, I had to pray for my ex-husband day and night. That was not easy, especially when he made it clear that he wanted me dead.

On top of that, the minute you claim to trust God you will immediately be put to the test. Know that when God is doing the testing, it is for your own good and will make you strong. Your faith will be tested as you grow. That goes for all of God's children. God is always striving to get us somewhere, but some of us keep going the wrong way. So He has to redirect us so we won't miss his plan for our lives.

For instance, when we start to take matters in our own hands and move a perfect stranger in to our house, we are operating out of loneliness or desperation — and are NOT operating within God's "best" for us. Then we have the nerve to blame God? Yet when we walk in the anointing of trusting God, we do not waver when trouble comes. We become unmovable and change not. God's desire is that we walk in His confidence and know that He has everything under control. Most of all, He desires that you trust Him. I pray that what this scripture has done for me will also do the same for you. Be blessed. Trust God.

Trusting God:

Do not fret because of evildoers, nor be envious of the workers of iniquity, for they shall soon be cut down like the grass. Moreover, wither as the green herb. Trust in the Lord and do well. Dwell in the land and feed on His faithfulness. Delight yourself also in the Lord and he shall give you the desires of your heart; commit your way to the Lord, trust also Him and he shall bring it to pass. He shall bring forth your righteous as the night and your justice as the noonday. Rest in the Lord and wait patiently for Him. Do not fret because of him who prospers in his way because of the man who brings wicked schemes to pass, cease from anger and forsake wrath, do not fret it only causes harm. For evildoers shall be cut off, but those who wait on the Lord they shall inherit the earth. In addition, shall delight them in the abundance of peace. The wicked plots against the just a gnashes at him with teeth. The Lord laughs at him for He sees his day is coming. The wicked have drawn the sword and have bent their bow to cast down poor and needy to slay those who are upright conduct. Their sword shall enter their own heart and their bows shall be broken. A little that a righteous man has is better than the riches of many wicked. For the arms of wicked shall be broken. However, the Lord upholds the righteous. The Lord knows the days of the upright and their inheritance shall be forever. They shall not perish and the enemies of the Lord like the splendor of meadows shall vanish into smoke they shall vanish away. The wicked borrows and does not repay, but the righteous show mercy and gives. For those blessed by Him shall inherit the earth. Nevertheless, those cursed by Him shall be cut off. The steps of a good man are ordered by the Lord upholds him with His hand. Depart from evil and do well, and dwell forevermore. For the Lord loves justice and does not forsake his saints. They are preserved forevermore. However, the descendants of the wicked shall be cut off. The righteous shall inherit the land and dwell in forever. The mouth of the righteous speaks wisdom, and his tongue talks of justice. The law of his God is in his heart, none of his steps shall slide. The wicked watches the righteous and seeks to slay him. The Lord will not leave him in his hand, nor condemn him when he is judged. Wait on the Lord, keep his way and he shall exalt you to inherit the land. When the wicked are cut off, you shall see it. I have seen the wicked in great power, and spreading himself like a native green tree, yet he passed away and behold, he was no more, indeed I sought him but he could not be found. Mark the blameless man and observe the upright for the future of that man is peace but the transgressors shall be destroyed together. The future of the wicked shall cut off. But the salvation of the righteous from the Lord He is their strength in the time of trouble, and the Lord shall help them and deliver them, He shall deliver them from the wicked and save them because they trust in Him. -- Psalm 37 (Amp version)

PRAISE AND WORSHIP

I believe there is a special place in God's heart for praise and worship. The Bible tells us that God delights in it, and likewise anointed music is one of the greatest gifts God has given us to enjoy. When we enter in, a beautiful time between you and the Lord commences. It's so glorious that at times I would go to sleep at night with music in my ear.

During this season of writing, I took my television out of my room and only listened to anointed Christian music. Previously, I would watch a television show late at night (I like comedy), but lately I have only needed a couple of favorite CD's to play. I felt myself drawn to praise and worship music and recommend it for the soul! I suggest you stop everything and let the music draw you into a state of praise and worship. There is an awesome anointing that comes with your personal praise and worship time alone with the Lord at home; it is not the same as in church. This is a time you can let it all out. You can dance, sing, or just quietly sit before the Lord and reverence Him by telling Him how much you love and appreciate what He's done for you. You can sob and weep. You can rejoice and laugh. He will take you to a place where nothing else matters except for you and Him.

It is one of the most beautiful experiences you will ever have. It will open the heart of God every time. You will begin to realize that you are not alone nor forsaken. Praise and worship sets the atmosphere for the anointing to show up, and your circumstances become smaller and smaller during this time. You will get answers you never thought of before. This is the place you strive for and may never want to leave from. It's just that wonderful.

REMEMBER:

1.) It's OKAY TO CRY, 2.) YOU CAN LET GO, and 3.) TRUST GOD.

You will begin to see your circumstance change right before your eyes during this precious time of fellowship and union with

God. He is beginning a work in you without you even knowing it, and all it takes is spending time doing something you love doing anyway — praise and worship. The mountain that you saw is no longer a mountain anymore, and things are changing, and you are changing. You'll start liking it the benefits of praise and won't be able to wait to do it again.

The born-again spirit within you is enjoying every minute of its awakening. It is no longer asleep and it longs to fellowship with God's spirit... it is set up that way and is best compared to the birth of a newborn baby who immediately gravitates to the breast. The minute we are born again, we began to pull toward God's heart. And just as the newborn needs to be fed multiple times every day, so our spirit yearns to be fed.

In praise and worship, we open our mouth and utter praises, and combined with reading the scripture we become strong and healthy Christians, inside and out. You get an instant response from God because it pleases Him and He loves it. It will automatically take you to another level. Loving Him with all your heart, mind, soul and strength opens the door for many blessings to flow. So if you are praising and worshipping God, get ready to be blessed. God loves blessing his people when He is pleased.

I cannot say enough about praise and worship. I can go on and on. The moment you break through and worship God in spirit and in truth, you are a threat to the devil. Now you are in God's perfect will. This is a weapon given to us so that we can be successful in our daily walk. Start doing it and watch your day go by in victory. Put your "praise on" and dance and get caught up in Him — the one you love the most. He is the lover of your soul and there is none greater than He. Your praise and worship tells God how you really feel about Him.

We have been redeemed, so let the redeemed of the Lord say so. Do you love Jesus today? Then say so. Let the enemies know who you are and that you are not ashamed of the Gospel of Christ. Then put on the praise and worship music all day and night until you get released and the stress passes. Listen to Christian tapes, read your Bible and look at Christian videos — anything that can give God Glory. That's how you get a victory over the devil.

HARD TIMES

THERE is no way you are going to run this race without going through some hard times. Let's face the truth and be real. Even though hard times come, it is not quicksand. You are not meant to stay stuck and have a pity party. Certainly, when things happen to us, we hurt. Just remember that the trials will come, and what determines if you will stand or not is... YOU.

Sometimes life hurts. That's what makes the love of God such a relief. Know that as you go through the storms you are not alone. This is the time for you to draw from what God has placed inside of you. Just think of it as a test, and it's one that you can pass. It is time for baby bird to leave its mother's nest on a trial run. Let's see how well you handle it. Will you lose it, or grab hold of what God has bestowed upon you? By the way, I know exactly how you feel. It feels like God is nowhere to be found, yet once in a while God will place a word on another saint's heart to remind you that He still cares and loves you just the same.

Hard times is not a location. You are not meant to take up residence there. Rather, hard times are meant to groom you for greater works. Every Christian goes there for a time to be prepared for future missions, plans, journeys, adventures and callings. Honestly, as I went through my "hard times" I was more interested in how was God going to come through. Normally I don't want people to see this side of me, because I'd rather them see the faith side (where I'm fully trusting God). But I have learned its okay to be honest with God and say, "God, I have no idea how you are going to make this work on my behalf." I also finish my comment with, "Nevertheless, I trust you."

I thought very seriously about Abraham's test to sacrifice his only son. Thank God he passed it! God wants us all to pass, but He realizes we are going to miss it at times. Someone once told me there are only two times you should pray. 1.) When you feel like it, and 2.) And when you don't feel like it. I believe it's when we don't feel like it that God honors our prayers the most. Try it and see. Stay with it for one hour and see that "something" wants to change — some mountain wants to move.

For me, Psalm 37 worked miracles in my life every time. Each verse means something to me and I held on to them all as if my life depended upon it, especially the first month post-divorce. Toward the end of that month, Psalm 37 started to work even more. I knew is it was out of question to give up, because I was determined and armed with the word of God. Even though at times I didn't think these trials would ever end, they did. And it turns out that God was true to His word.

No matter what it looks like, my advice is to trust God completely through the hard times. It seemed very difficult for me to get through the early months after the divorce, especially my problems with sleeping and eating. It even hurt to think about it, and perhaps you feel this way, as well. Sometimes you may need professional help from a counselor to move on, and in my case it certainly helped. There is also an additional counselor who can help... and this one does not rent space in an office building. No, this counselor abides within you. The Holy Spirit is your friend, and you can also find strength and courage in Proverb 20:5, which says, "Counsel in the heart of man is like deep water; but a man of understanding will draw it out."

I wanted to share real experiences with you. Sweet women of God, you may be going through the most terrible experience imaginable — a divorce you either wanted or didn't want at all. Oh, the tearing that takes place in the spirit can consume you, especially if you still love your husband. Perhaps you don't care if you just found out he has a girlfriend and baby on the way. Perhaps he's beaten you senseless, yet you still love him. Perhaps he's failed miserably as a provider and partner, yet even after all he has put you through, you still pine for him. Perhaps he left you with nothing, stole everything, and regardless you continue to do nothing but love him.

God wants to fill that space with a new love, His love, that will never fail you. Get alone in a quiet place and let God began to fill that space in your heart that has been torn open.

True, it can be very humiliating to go through hard times. People who have not walked in your shoes may not believe it can be that bad. That's why I had to write this book. People need to know and learn to empathize. Even with everything going on with you right now, I say to you this day: "YOU ARE GOING TO MAKE IT!"

LIFE STILL GOES ON

YOU have to wake up and smell the coffee. The kids need you, and life doesn't stop on a dime just because you are facing a relationship meltdown. You must do something. You can't just sit there without putting in an effort. There are gifts that God has placed inside of you, so use everything you have to the Glory of God.

No matter what you are going through, it cannot be worse than death. Stay encouraged and find a way to turn the negative into a positive. You are not alone. You cannot afford to have a pity party. Too many other people need you, and on top of that God has a purpose for you. Your life and your journey are valuable. YOU are valuable. Say out loud, "I am going to make it because God is on my side!"

You may need to give yourself a little push. Try making the Bible your best friend. What I found helpful was reading confessions out of the Bible. Make up in your mind that you are not going to take this lying down, and that you will utilize God's own tool — the Bible — to hope and cope. Tell yourself, "If I made it through all of the abusive words, I can make it through this." Or remind yourself, "I refuse to go out like that." Or encourage someone else by saying, "I lived through it, and you are going to make it too!"

I am so used to encouraging my family and keeping them upbeat. It's a real blessing when your children notice and emulate your example. Our children will sometimes turn the tables on us and remind us to be encouraged. We really need to listen to what they have to say. Just because we are the parent it doesn't mean we know everything. Once my daughter reminded me of a phrase I once said to her: "This thing is not about you." Once she spoke those words to me, and I caught them. Even though I said it to her many times, I needed to be reminded.

I will tell you now that this is true; this thing is not about you, so get over it. This life of yours is too precious to waste away. You are special in God's sight. Once it dawned on me that if I didn't choose to do something positive in my life, no one else would either. Notice how people go about their business whether you are in or out. Likewise, you can choose today to go on with your life whether a man has opted in or out. There are significant challenges that people face every day, and the final decision is yours. You cannot stay where you are, trapped in "I can't."

Do not even think about taking your life. You are living through a temporary circumstance — emphasis on temporary. Keep on keeping on... and remember that this, too, shall pass. Take your mind off you and start thinking about somebody else, because you are not the only one who is suffering. Many women have gone through worse. It is not the end of the world, so snap out of it and go on. This truly is something we must do for ourselves, and you cannot continue to hide and let your life pass you by.

Sure, people can be cruel and inconsiderate about what you are going through. You can't stop people from treating you this way. You can't allow other people's opinions, judgment or stupidity to rule your universe. For instance, I wanted everyone to experience my pain and empathize with me, especially my children. I wanted them, at least, to understand — especially since no everyone else did. However, in hindsight that only put pressure on them. I wasn't purposely doing it, but that's what happened. Just because our lives have been altered, why mess up theirs? Life still goes on, so let them live theirs while you find yours.

CHAPTER TWO

IN A TIME OF DESPAIR

DURING the first year that went through my divorce, it felt as if I was the only one. Something that I cherished very much — my prayer life — was under attack. I had problems praying and just didn't feel like it, so days went by and all I could say every day was, "Thank you, Jesus."

Yet I am spiritual enough to know how important prayer is, and I knew what would happen if I didn't get my prayer life back. I would get on my computer and send prayer requests to other prayer ministries and 24/7/365 prayer warriors. That is one of the best pieces of advice I can share: surround yourself with people who will pray for you. We already know how to say, "Thank you, Jesus," but we all need a little more than that.

During this time, all you may see is darkness. For heaven's sake, don't just sit there. Don't be ashamed to ask for help and cry out! Ask God to have someone come into your life who will pray with you when you ask him or her, someone who is not afraid to pray. You need a Holy Ghost, tongue-talking, Bible-walking warrior to go in and fight on your behalf.

Eventually I was blessed with everything I needed. Notice that I did not say, "everything I wanted." No, I received what I needed, and found that God had already made it available for me in His good timing. He is a God who has all the bases covered, and nothing is lacking. So without a doubt, you will leave this place of unhappiness and move on. You are here on earth to do something special for yourself that ministers to others, as well. I discovered that something as simple as polishing my own nails was a ministry, of sorts. I kept my nails clean, trimmed and polished, because that meant something to me and it didn't cost anything. Oddly, it caught people's attention. People didn't realize I was doing them myself and could not afford to have my nails done, let alone put gas in my car. This was my secret, and I did not tell anyone.

After noticing my nails, many people would ask me time and time again, "Where exactly do you work?" Well, I work at home taking care of my grandkids. It doesn't take much too pretty up my nails and proves that it's the little things that count. God will take whatever you have and use it. He delights in you during the good times and bad. You see, God started developing me into another person, one that was ready and equipped for anything that came my way. That old person died along with my marriage. If I had completely trusted in God, my path would have been easier. But I continued to rebel because I wasn't ready to move on yet.

So what I am saying is, God will allow you to wallow in your sadness until you are ready to move on. He is a gentleman and will not override your will. But once I found His perfect will, I started a completely new way of life. I became concerned about what I was eating and how I looked. Since the fingernail polish worked so well, I decided to change in other areas.

I started getting interested in exercise. I am a very small person, but I needed to tone up a little here and there. Exercise became part of my new existence and was something I could never do before. But eventually my arms, legs and chest toned up. Then my diet was another concern. When you are 48 and about to be single, you want to look and feel your best — not for anyone else, but for yourself.

Now, I didn't get crazy with the new look. I only changed a few basic things. Selecting the right foods to eat ministered to my entire family down to my grandchildren. Whenever I went somewhere with my son or daughter, people's faces dropped when I was introduced as their mother. This happened every time, and it was simply because I exercised mildly and ate thoughtfully. Other times when I went to my grandchildren's school and introduced myself to their teachers. Their faces also registered surprise. Men started to look at me — my daughter always noticed such things even when I didn't — and kept an eye out for me, even offering good advice for the first steps in my new single life.

HOW DO YOU GO ON?

MY divorce put such a fear in me about men. How could I ever think about stepping into a relationship again? My counselor's advice was to wait one year after my divorce before dating. That was fine with me! With my mindset, I could wait forever and dating was the furthest thing from my mind. After coming close to being murdered by my husband (the man who said he loved me) I was more than ready to hang it all up. If it were left up to me, I would choose never to date again.

Even though it was proven later on that my husband had a nervous breakdown, nevertheless the abuse still happened. But I could not get stuck there in that dark history of my life. Yet I had no idea what to do next. So I just lived one day at a time. Soon things got better, but it was not a quick fix. There are choices in life and also consequences that many of us don't consider until it's too late.

As I look back now, I can't blame anyone but myself. Now I'm learning each day that I can't go back and "undo" what has already happened. But we can forgive ourselves just as we forgive others. What's done is done, and we should not dwell on it. I try my best to think positively most of the time, and I am still learning as I go along. It may be a good idea to take the attention off of you and focus on your friendships and family ties with others.

I recently went to lunch with a woman from church for the third time. The first two times she treated me, but this particular time I was able to treat her. I had noticed that she talked about herself a lot, whereas I didn't say anything. By the third time, I realized something else was going on. Her need was not financial or a hurting marriage. Can you guess what her need was? You guessed it! She just needed someone to listen. It was also a chance for me to sharpen my listening skills. It was my opportunity to bless someone else by lending an ear.

As you move on, it helps to remember to reach out and help others by giving of yourself. Just cherish where you are right now and make the best of it. Do not rush it, for in due season your time will come and you will find yourself happy and fulfilled. It's a process.

ALL ALONE

I had already made up in my mind that I would be alone for the rest of my life, and I was fine with that. One day I was reading the Bible, and 2 Corinthians jumped out at me. Paul spoke of how happy he was not ever being married. I thought to myself, "Well, that's just what I am going to do. I can live without sex for the rest of my life."

Our bedroom marriage was not the best. I thought for sure something was wrong with me and I needed help, or at least this is what my husband used to tell me. We decided we needed to talk to a professional — someone who could understand where we were coming from. Of course, by all means I insisted the counselor had to be Christian.

Well, it turned out that our counselor was a husband and wife team. The first appointment was a disaster. My husband immediately convinced the marriage counselors that something was wrong with me. To my amazement, they agreed with him. He was so convincing that even I believed him. Nevertheless, I want to take just a few minutes to say: ladies, it is not your fault. In my case I found out later my husband was sleeping with another woman and comparing me to her. He was so good at fooling people it didn't surprise me that the counselors fell for it.

God wants you to have a mate who loves you and adores you, and only you, the way He does. That is why He wants you to wait on Him. Could it be possible that your "failed" mate may not have been the one God had planned for you? Being unequally yoked can (and does) cause major problems.

After I studied the chapter about Paul, I felt happy knowing I would be okay with or without a mate. I didn't have to worry about a man ever hurting me again. But before I could get comfortable with that statement, God spoke to my heart and confronted me; I heard these words in my spirit: "There is a mate I have especially for you." This thought out of nowhere appeared in my mind, and I began to weep. Then I remember saying, "Lord, no, I cannot bear to go through this again!" Then I had the most comforting confidence in my spirit assuring me I would not be alone, and that God, Himself, would send me the right mate next time.

After that I was never afraid of being alone again. This made me love God even more. Just to know that He had me on His mind was all I needed at the time. I continued studying the Bible. Proverbs 3:10-18 resonated as I read about the endeavors of virtuous women. I also read books about marriage and family.

Months had passed before I got another panic attack, and this one had me thinking about everything that had gone on during my separation. More panic attacks followed, and it became worse and worse each time. I kept questioning myself and asking God, "Why did this have to happen?" I had tried so hard, and my marriage still failed. We promised each other we would always be together always… but we didn't. Now I was feeling all alone.

Because I moved to another state, I didn't know what happened to him. I got my divorce papers in the mail four months later and it was over. In theory, all I had to do is get over it and move on. But as many of you know, it's not that easy. We had some business connections together and a few other things, which made it hard for me to concentrate and be rational. So without thinking I gave it all up, took the loss, accepted my part in our debt, and then tried to move on.

This is when I really was all alone — being broke and feeling disgusted. The last thing I need is for someone to say, "Now, if you need anything just let me know." Are they serious, or what? Sure, I needed something! My whole life had just turned upside down, and this is all they could come up with? Do not get me started, because I could go on about insincere remarks. Chances are, it has happened to you just as it happened to me. I had people coming up to me telling me crazy stuff. I believe they meant well, or at least I will give them the benefit of the doubt. But did they truly think I had it all under control just because I was not looking ugly enough?

Christian women, women who love God with all their hearts, go through this stuff and need you to pray for them. Be a blessing in their lives, just like that drug addict you picked up off the street. Please, if you know of anyone going through a divorce, I beg you don't pass them by just because they look like they have it together. Let me spell it out for you. As I stated before, women facing divorce need something other than prayer. It's called money. Be a financial blessing and write them a check. Even though it's not the cure for everything (because they still have a long way to go), it sure helps them feel not so alone.

MY REFUGE

WHEN I think of refuge, I recall how I got away from my abusive marriage without being harmed. Sure, I was emotionally battered, but I was still alive. My spirit, body and relationship with God were still intact. I thank God for my two children coming to my rescue, and even in the process my daughter got her foot broken trying to defend me in a fight with my husband. Besides that, she had nightmares about him coming to kill the entire family.

My husband could bully me and get away with it, but when it came to the children, well, he was afraid of them. He knew that they loved me and would do anything to protect me. It hurt me more than anything to see how my children suffered through all the pain my marriage caused, especially due to the decisions my husband and I made. After my children realized that I was safe and away from it all, they were happy. I think the best decision I made was moving to another state away from my marriage, my home, and the business. I really believe if I had stayed I would not be writing this book or even be here today.

I had to quietly leave town without letting anyone know. I knew if my husband found out, he would try and hurt me in some way because he had already broken into the house and left a dead bird in the middle of my floor. It seemed he just snapped, and my formerly sweet husband turned into a monster. He started watching those strange detective shows and then tried to reenact the scenes in real life. I filed a restraining order against him, but not even that kept him away from me. Who knows what he would try next? I was not about to stay around and find out.

It was time for me to go when my son left Japan and returned to the States. An opportunity for a move to Florida was open, and I took it. Off to the Sunshine State I went. But once I decided to leave, everyone I knew turned against me. They all thought I was losing it, except my two children. Family members and friends each had their own opinion as to why I should stay. All of their ideas seemed to be better than mine. They actually thought I had not sought God for myself and had not received "divine" permission to leave. I realize I had let these people control me and not God. Doubters, skeptics and naysayers aside, the bottom line is: anyone in this situation is going to need refuge from God and God alone.

Of course, my children did not fully grasp the condemnation, nor did they completely comprehend my compulsion to move. It was hard for them to understand why I did what I did, and they didn't "get" why I didn't want anything to do with these people anymore. I felt bad that the kids had to go through it with me. Still, I was determined to completely remove myself from all the disapproval and believed God for my future. Once I allowed God to cut away anything and anyone who was not for me, I was prepared to stay away for the rest of my life if it took that.

God knows when something is not right for you. He will cut it away Himself. It may be family, friends or fellow Christians. They may claim to have all the answers about your life when their own is messed up worse than yours, so do not let them fool you. They are not little gods in your life. God is your only God and refuge, and you can draw from him the shelter you need. Let him protect you from the wolves out there. Be obedient to Him no matter what.

CHAPTER THREE

ENDLESS LOVE

FOREVER and ever, Oh Lord, I will always love you. The love we have for God should always remain, just as his love for us is unwavering. From the moment I was saved in 1994, I fell in love with Jesus and still am. This love walk outweighs anything the world has to offer.

Even after a failed marriage, God still loves us, and this love continues to develop our character. So even when someone has done you wrong, maintain your good character and don't bow down to their level. Walk in unconditional love (agape love) — the same way God drew you to Him through love and kindness. It does not cost anything to be nice to people, so keep a smile on your face and mean it. When your ways please the Lord, that is all that matters. He can take care of the rest and cause even your enemies to be at peace with you. The peace that God gives you is better than anything you can ever imagine.

Most people feel uncomfortable regarding the area I am about to address. But real love from God brings about intimacy. When you love someone, you want to spend private time with them with the door closed. This tells God how you really feel about Him when it is only you and Him. Began to get to that place where you can love Jesus. Let Him hold you and love on you all night long without you saying a word. You will start to notice that the circumstances around you are smaller in His presence, you will not care anymore about the trauma and drama; all you will care about is Him, and resting in His presence.

This new love will make you do things you have never done before. You will have a sense of overwhelmingly happiness all the time, and won't be able to wait to read your Bible again (and won't want to put it down). People may be puzzled by your joy and may even ask what is wrong with you. They will talk amongst themselves to try and figure out what has made you different.

As a new believer I was very excited about the things happening in my life. If I was led to do something, I didn't think twice and was not ashamed at all. I just did it. As I grew as a Christian I continued to love on God and honor Him in everything and with everything in me. Of course I wasn't perfect, but I was certainly passionate about being the Christian woman I knew God wanted me to be.

This was evident as I worked as a private home care provider for the elderly. On one particular assignment a woman said to me, "I want what you have!" She had been depressed for years, and her daughter had taken her to all kinds of doctors. She was put on different types of medications and organic foods. Nothing worked... until I came along.

The elderly woman began watching me and told her daughter about my enthusiasm and faith. After that, the daughter asked a lot of questions about my Christian walk. She made it clear that she was the "real Christian" and was also the one who was paying me. Without even trying, I watched this daughter's heart change. Over a period of four years it manifested and came into full bloom. At the end of my acquaintance with this 84-year-old mother and her 60-year-old daughter, their family had healed. The daughter made amends with her three sisters and the mother received Christ into her heart. One year later she passed away after transforming from a depressed old woman into a peaceful soul. Often she would ask me to pray for her and afterward made me promise I would be with her until the end when she passed away.

That promise was kept. I was standing by her bedside as my friend took her last breath and transcended into Heaven. Until you actually face death, you may not be sure what love can do for somebody else. In the case of this elderly lady, she prayed to have a relationship with God like I had. Now the rest of her family is indeed grateful for the relationship I nurtured with their mother, which was carried out all the way to the end. With all the thank you cards, money and gifts they gave me, nothing beat the best gift of all, which was sharing the love I had for God. There was no way I could hide my zeal for Him no matter how hard I tried!

Soon word got around and my phone started ringing. Calls were coming from other families wanting me to visit their mother and loved ones. That was evidence that my love of God was still having a ripple effect. It had spread like wildfire from me to my elderly friend, and now to others. I looked at God's love as a gift that just keeps on giving, and it was He who was doing the leading and the changing.

What I had tapped into was a part of God that most people never find. I know, because I ask many people about their love walk, and they don't seem to understand what I am talking about. All I know is this: I remember one of my sisters once told me that I didn't have any compassion. My Dad was in the hospital at the time and I was sitting in the chair waiting for the nurse to bring him back in his room. I began to read my Bible, and my sister came in the room shouting, "Put the Bible down! Don't you see that our Dad could be in there dying, and all you can do is sit there and read?" That's when she informed me that I didn't have any compassion.

Those words went straight through me. I thought about what she said, and after she calmed down I asked what she meant by that statement. She went on to say, as I listened closely, "There is a time to read the Bible and a time to put it down and do something." She continued, "You've done all the reading, so now do something!" That is when I made up in my mind that I was going to do something.

So the first thing I did was, of course, go to the Bible and read the scriptures showing Jesus having compassion. A special passage, after the news of His cousin John the Baptist's death, says, "He went up to pray and as he returned he saw all the people standing, and his heart was filled with compassion for the people."

That's it! That's what I want!

Right then I asked God to bless me with the same compassion exemplified by Jesus. My sister didn't realize that by angrily shouting at me, a light came on in my spirit and changed my life. Well, I must tell you that I got what I prayed for — compassion. I began an obsession with Jesus and simply could not get enough. It was Jesus morning, noon, and night, and this went on and on.

I love Him and everything about Him. I love people, especially older people. People in nursing homes all seemed to want me around to pray for them. They became my friends. I was so addicted to God that no one could take His love from me. Instead, it poured out of me and all I wanted to do is share this blessed relationship with the Almighty. I talked to Him and He talked to me. He romanced me and I loved every minute of it.

Things were moving so fast, I thought something was wrong with me. But I realized it could only be one of two things: 1.) I was going crazy, or 2.) God really loved me! Since I was not going crazy, the truth was that God really did love me, and He is the same God who loves you, as well. He longs to fellowship with you and provides the love you have been searching for all your life. It's the endless, fulfilling kind of love that will never end.

TAKE YOUR TIME

TAKE your time. You have just come through a terrible experience. Do not expect to bounce back at the snap of a finger. It truly takes time, so don't rush it. Relax for a minute and, if possible, do not hurry back into work. If you have paid vacation coming, now is a good time to use it.

We live in a microwave society. We expect everything to be "instant." Right after my separation, I wanted a quick divorce and I could not wait. I thought getting a divorce sooner would help eliminate some of the pain. But I have found no quick way to avoid pain. You will make it through by taking your time. Do not let anyone rush you before you are ready. I chose not to go to nightclubs or date. That was not what I wanted to do, but I personally do not ever want to "play God." Instead, I want to focus on just "doing me." Everyone is different and there is nothing wrong if your choices vary from mine. Just be sure you are on the path God has constructed for you. Stay in His will, even during the most desperate of times.

My kids tell me I am too serious at times, but I label my salvation as a serious matter. I just cannot forget what God has done for me. He took my place on the cross and went through terrible things just for me. That alone is enough to keep me steadfast.

People do not think you can have fun and be saved at the same time. Yet I have fun being saved and have plenty to do. If you need to find an activity, start with your church or listen to your local Christian radio station for ideas. And, in my case, there were always my children and grandchildren. My son worked nearby and stopped by every day to see how I was doing. He was very good during all of this transition and always made sure that I was taken care of, no matter what. As he greeted me each day his first response was to give me a hug, then ask, "What did you do today?" As I went down my list, it consisted of reading my Bible, praying, cooking cleaning, taking care of the kids... and writing my book. He listened with an open ear, God bless him.

As you take your time and wait on God, focus on doing for others. Psalm 37:21 talks about being generous to others, so consider reaching outside of your comfort zone and taking someone to dinner. Do little project that will keep you motivated. I volunteered to do jail ministry on Saturday mornings with a group I met at Church.

And although it's tempting, do not keep telling everyone about your divorce repeatedly. I heard someone say once that if you keep talking about your past it may end up being your future. Take your time with friends and be very selective. The few people God allowed me to meet knew very little about me. The area I lived in was generally family or military. It is not a good idea to be around gossip or nosy people, so please do not let anyone diminish the work God is doing in you. You have come too far to let foolishness rip away your joy!

You will get back into the swing of things, even better than before. Determine in your mind every day that you are going to make it. Do not accept the failures of the past and have a great expectation for your future. Prepare for success and keep yourself looking good. Do not let yourself go. Just as you kept your children looking neat and clean, you do this for yourself. Do it for you, because you deserve it.

Decent, empathetic people will know you do not have it all together yet, nor will they expect you to. Be real and make the best out of what you have. Thank God that you have made it this far, and that your children are safe. Forget about that ex-husband; let him be your children's Daddy, but not yours. Do not waver back and forth, or visit back and forth. Respect yourself and respect him. If it is over, it is truly over. You may not be able to be his friend right now, but keep on praying and allow God to deal with the matter.

Give God something to work with. Be kind to your ex and stay in right standing with God. Be honest. Tell God how you feel and what you want changed in your life. God certainly understands the feelings you are having. He is also going to deal with you first, especially if you have done wrong. So be honest and do not blame your ex-husband unjustly. God desires to clean house and make you into brand new being, a reinvigorated, virtuous women — someone He can use. What a perfect time to prepare yourself for your one true love, Jesus.

You are still a bride and you have a holy Savior as the love of your life. You did not fail. Rather, the marriage failed, so relax and take your time. You belong to someone and He is keeping you in a penthouse suit waiting for the right moment to deploy you on His path for your life. He will put you where you are supposed to be. People will notice something different about you, because you have been kept in the secret palace of the Most High God.

Now my prayer is, "Please Lord, do not let me think too highly of myself than I ought to, and do not let me be conceited to the point that people hate to see me coming. Now Lord, I thank you that I delight myself in you and you will give me the desires of my heart."

If you have not had much patience in your life, this can be difficult. It may be hard for you to relax, and you might be the type of person who always needs to be doing something. That happens, especially if all the children are gone and you have an empty nest. You are developing a new person inside, someone you never knew before. Something may come out of you that you never thought possible, so be ready for change. Change is a good thing.

Be aware that people and family may not be ready for the new you. Although I took a lot of criticism about the various decisions I made, thanks be to God that I made those choices.

CUTTING OLD TIES

CUTTING old ties is not easy. In fact, it is one of the hardest things I ever had to do. Because of what God was doing in my life, I came to realize I had to let go of certain people and make a change. Cutting old ties usually involves the people who are closest to you, for example, family, friends, co-workers and even Pastors.

I had accumulated what is called a soul tie. What is a soul tie? It's when the emotions, mind and will of a person become entangled to the point that their thoughts are no longer their own. In other words, it is co-dependency, which is an ungodly soul tie. No matter how hard you try, you will never be able to change this dependency on your own. That is why we need God to help us. People can be very cruel, and the ones you thought were for you seem to have turned against you. You will have to launch out and trust God. If God is doing the cutting, you can rest assured that He is doing it for a good reason. We are like trees being pruned. He is doing it on our behalf so that He may be glorified in all things. Let me warn you that it is going to hurt, but you will get over it. Be firm and stand your ground.

Although it would be easy to give up while you are going through this, God is doing a good work in you. Do not walk away from it in fear of hurting others. Just remember, obedience is better than sacrifice.

Cutting old ties brings out a lot of hurt feelings and emotions. You have just made a decision that you are no longer putting up with the same old stuff. What you are now doing is allowing God to cut away all the dead pieces of your life so that you can assume a new identity. Let Him cut all the dead branches away, and then allow Him to sculpt you into a vision of His own making.

Change is never easy. We get so use to having a generic lifestyle, never embracing change, and going to church for years without getting any further than the seat on the back row. Occasionally you might help in the kitchen, but other than that, how can God use you if all you want to do is sit in church and do absolutely nothing?

People, we have to grow up and shake off our apathy if we want to be used by God. Break away from the traditional and customary. Instead, do it God's way. Custom says, "Well, I am going to this church because this is the church I grew up in." Or perhaps you think, "Momma and Daddy went there, so if it was good enough for them, it is good enough for me." If old customs are taking you away from God, then you need to break tradition.

Yes, you have to take the risk of not being popular. People are going to talk and it won't be pretty. For instance, my Pastor is one of the greatest men of God I know. Yet people have said hurtful things about him. Now, I am sure God has already prepared him so his mind was ready for the cutting away and the change. Sometimes God may bring these same people back around again, and sometimes they are cut away forever. Please remember, when they come back it won't be the same... because you are different. Hopefully they are, as well.

It seems that by the time you finish cleaning house and ridding yourself of all the excess bondage, there is nothing left except you and God. Draw from Him everything you need. He is a mother, a father, a brother, a sister and a friend — your everything.

So, at this point I had reached what I refer to as my half way mark. My counselor called it "my fork in the road." I had gone too far to turn around. If you have gotten this far, then you are doing well — still saved, walking with the Lord, being obedient, and serving while you are waiting, being submissive to God, and still loving the Lord more than ever.

God is going to honor you. You passed the test! The following ideas will let you know that you have reached this milestone and are going to make it:

Have not given up on God

Remain pure in heart

Forgiven ex-husband

Love God with all your heart

Time is passing very quickly and you no longer need to hold on to strife or unforgiveness. Cut the cord and watch God work. Cutting old ties brings endless possibilities and fertile new ground in which you can bloom. It is time for new things; you are starting a new chapter in your life. Be encouraged and know you are not defeated. You are going to make it.

Be warned, though, that when people see you want a better life for yourself, they tend to hold on harder. They may make it more difficult for you by fabricating lies to keep you tied to them. They have accepted defeat and do not know why you have to break the mold. Now they see an opportunity to make a move, especially when they start to feel uncomfortable around you. You are reminding them that they need change in their lives, and if they are not ready for that change it can be frightening.

They may be facing their own dilemmas. Perhaps their husbands are cheating and they are putting up with it. So they may question why you want to get out. I had women get angry with me because I refuse to be abused mentally or physically any longer. I had people "inform" me that God had told them how I should "act" concerning my marriage. Just think, if I would have believed and listened to them, I might be dead.

Everyone has an opinion about what you should do. Don't listen to them and instead lean on God. Believe what He is telling you. I prayed and asked God one night to please take me out of all the abuse. I heard in my spirit, "No." So I waited, and a few months later I prayed that same prayer again. I knew my patience put me in sync with God's timing. I know it was God who rescued me, and I do not regret praying that prayer. I thank God for answering it. I am alive today, and more than my marriage ended that night: I cut away all the old, toxic ties.

CHAPTER FOUR

PROTECT YOURSELF

How do we protect ourselves from being hurt again? I found there is no way we can do this by ourselves. Trusting God is the only protection you will ever need. The devil does not play fair, and every time you think you have things figured out something new will take you by surprise. So don't even try to figure it all out. Lay all that aside and just say, "Lord, I am going to trust you."

You can try and protect yourself, but in my experience it won't work. I went to my counselor and asked him, "Now tell me, since my marriage has failed and I got hurt very badly, how can I protect myself from this happening to me again?" He laughed and said, "There are no guarantees that this won't happen again." How disappointing! I felt sure he was going to give me a formula — you know — steps to follow to a tee. It was horrifying to realize there was no man-made solution, and to go through abuse again would be like death to me. The only sure fire solution is God's solution.

I thought to myself, "Lord, I am 48 years old and have been divorced for less than a year. What shall I do now?" Then came another big question in my life: "What shall I do about sex?" I did not want to be hurt again and was ready to give up sex for the rest of my life. By now, I knew all of this was bigger than I was and there was no way I could figure it all out alone.

When I looked at men, I had no interest whatsoever. I was content to be alone. I was not angry with men, but just didn't want to be bothered. I thought I had learned enough about marriage to last me a lifetime. It was a full time job keeping my guard up. I was thankful I had this time to learn about myself and all the gifts God had placed inside of me. I used it as an opportunity to find out more about my destiny and how I worked, and what choices I had. I knew that I was a nice person and I deserved to have someone love me, but I was not ready to dive back in for a while.

Someone told me about a program called True Love Waits. From what I heard about this program, it was exactly what I needed. There is a ceremony at the end of the program that includes you, your parents, your sponsor, or prayer partner. A promise ring is presented and you keep the ring on until you get married. Your husband is the first to take it off. It is designed for teenagers, but anyone can participate. I decided to do it and share the occasion with my family.

I have since gotten over the idea of never marrying again and I am now looking forward to it. Since we do a terrible job protecting ourselves, it is good to accept that God is much better at it than we are. I learned to trust God by first committing everything to Him, knowing He will give me all my heart's desires.

No matter how many times we say, "I do not want to get married again," we are just lying to ourselves. Every woman should want to be loved by a man... that man being her husband. We love it when our husbands look into our eyes and say, "I love you." Do not let fear or bitterness rob you of this love.

I recall that when I was a little girl, my father told me our family name was the original name from Nigeria, Africa. Our African ancestors were brought over by boat and landed in Virginia. Somehow, my great, great grandfather escaped to Alabama along with some of his brothers. They stayed hidden in the woods and made their homes in a small town called Latham. Therefore, I came from a lineage of fearful people. The goal of my African family was to protect themselves from the so-called white man and to keep from being captured.

This is just an example of extreme measures we are willing to take to protect ourselves, and also demonstrates how it can affect entire generations. Fear plays a great part in our destiny. By no means should we rely on the enemy to help us. However, God will help us and always gets the glory.

I am derived from my great, great, grandfather's ancestry — a man who thought he had won the victory over the white man. Yet he lived in fear for the rest of his life and passed that fear to his own children. I do not want fear to control anything that I do. Nor should you want it to be a part of your life.

I watched my Dad go through life believing in witchcraft and trying to protect himself the only way he knew how. When I got older and realized what was happening, I got very angry. But I soon realized that it was not his fault. He was only doing what his father had taught him, and that was how to keep away the white man (and anyone who was a threat). Building walls around our perfect little worlds won't work. It takes more than that.

You know you did not just "show up" on the earth. Someone had to create you. Be real and know that God is our creator and protector. When I try to protect myself, it's a temporary fix. It's like putting on a bandage until I can get to the doctor. When we get to the doctor, he takes off the bandage and cleans the wound out. This is what we need to let God do: clean the wound out and do surgery, if necessary. Begin to open yourself up and welcome the Holy Spirit into His dwelling place — your heart, mind and soul. He will protect you and keep you hidden in Christ. My family tried to do this on their own, and it caused fear to seep in.

A Prayer for You:

Dear Lord,

You are my protector and you know all things. Protect me from myself. I give this burden over to you now, in Jesus' name. I surrender this to God and will no longer try to protect myself. In Jesus' name, amen.

Now is a good time to have personal time alone and fellowship with God. It's a wonderful time to reflect and remember that we should never get in His way. I was wrong for trying to protect myself and hiding behind a huge wall where no one could enter. I felt God was saying to me, "Do not shut me out! There is someone I have for you."

I got so scared one day when I saw a beautiful vision in my mind of a bride coming down the aisle. I turned my head to see who was getting married, but instead of feeling happy I started to cry. I could hardly believe it, for it was me walking in that long white wedding gown. My heart started to flutter and I moved on to something else. I refuse to think about it any longer... but I knew God would bring this picture back into focus again.

I cried for days about it, just begging God, "Please, please, God! Do not let this happen again!" I thought I would be ready knowing God was in the equation, but I wasn't. The idea of marriage scared me to death. I wanted this thought to go away and never come back. I knew that God could see a part of my heart that I wanted to keep hidden. Somewhere I had buried a marriage and was prepared to keep it in a grave where it could not hurt me. Then I remembered the words: "He will give us all our heart's desires."

God can read your heart. Before I could write this book, God had to show me who I was, and everything I went through prepared me for this journey. At first thought I just got a bad deal for no reason. I believe my marriage continued only because both my husband and I needed to get material things. In short, anything that you write you will first experience. God knew I would come out of it safe so I could write this book — something I was born to write. I now believe He even looked further in the future to see the affect it would have on somebody else who has lived through a destructive relationship.

My marriage ended very abruptly, along with all my emotions, a few of my dreams, and most of my hope. I was devastated, because I previously assumed I would be someone who could write a bestseller on how to have a successful marriage! Now my own marriage was over and I was floored by the tragedy. One thing I was sure about was that I would never give up on my Lord Jesus Christ. I could not see myself without Him.

Daughter of God, the reason your husband has being blessed is because of you. Proverbs 18-22 says, "He who finds a wife finds a good thing and obtains favor from the Lord." There is favor in a wife if she's a good thing, and I believed I was a good thing. When my marriage went south, God had every intention on keeping me protected. There was nothing I could ever do to top that.

So just leave it alone. Stop fighting against God and let His will be done. He will not let you down. The entire Chapter of Psalm 37 was restful for me. I invite you to rest in it also. Let it do for you what it has done in my life. You will need it as you go to the next level. I heard a Pastor say that when he first got started in the Ministry, he had very little. Life as a man of God was actually a lot easier before he grew a larger ministry. Now things are much harder (meaning in a good way). I took it to mean he pressed on and pressed into what God had for him. That always requires more work. Where much is given, much is required. Now he has to pray more, fast more, and be more accountable.

God is also holding us accountable after we come into the full knowledge of our destiny. He expects us to walk in it. As Jesus returns, He will expect us to be in the place He has positioned us and graced us to be. Do not be caught in the wrong church or doing the wrong thing. Your judgment will have already been set. It will be too late for change. At times I could not see God anywhere in the picture, and it took a lot for me to know God had my back. I had to stop nourishing my wound; I had to take that bandage off and let God work on it. And so do you.

There was one thing I recall that made me realize God was present all along, and that was after realizing that I was still alive after being threatened with my life. I was not sure I was going to make it out alive, because there were demons living in my marriage and they were out to kill me. When that did not happen I knew it was God's tender loving arms protecting me.

Women of God just know that God has your back. Believe that, trust that, and know you will never find anyone that you can trust your life to other than God. All He wants to do is protect you. He will only allow so much, and will ensure that whatever you experience will help you in the long run. Make up in your mind that you are going through the wall, or around the wall, or over the wall, or under the wall. Let God tear the walls down or dig those escape routes a little at a time. Then He will replace your faint heart with a heart of warmth, decency, power and remarkable courage. Remind yourself every day that you are not carrying the burden any longer. God has redeemed and delivered you, so open your mouth and say something every day. You are bold, so claim your rights. You are changing and have the full knowledge of who is your shield; let the darts slide off of you.

I learned I could not write about something that I had not done myself... so if I can do it, so can you. You won't be concerned anymore about what people are saying. Do not try to figure them out. Analyze criticism and see if it lines up with your contract with God. You have a choice as to whether you want to receive it or not. You can decide to sign it, send back, return to sender, or forward to a new address. Now you have just allowed God to be your protector. He loves it, and it pleases the Lord to see you growing and depending on His word to get you through. This is one of your weapons, so use it to stay on top of things. Do not get beat up. Give the enemy a dose of his own medicine by staying behind God's perfect shield, which deflects the hurtful attacks.

I remember having an argument with my husband. I started to cry and he told me, "Shut up before I give you something to cry about." So give the enemy something to cry about. He's made you cry enough. You have to get to the point that you are sick and tired of being sick and tired. Read Phil: 4-13 and remember that you can do all things through Christ who strengthens you. Remember, it's not your strength, but God's. Do not take the credit; give God all the Glory because He is your Savior, your hero and your protector.

We move from faith to faith to glory to glory. While going through my divorce a lot of things were said that were not true. There were so many lies I could not keep up with them all, one right after the other. I stopped in the middle of it all and let people say whatever they wanted about me, while I said nothing. It would not have done any good anyway. All I remember thinking was, "Is the devil winning? No! I don't have to defend myself when I have God Almighty to do it for me!"

That was just what God wanted me to do — not to worry or do anything to save my reputation as it went down the drain. Why did I need to protect my reputation? I could not stop all those lies that were flying around me. Psalm 37:1 reminded me again that God is in control. This chapter spoke to me every day and was full of whatever I needed. I just went to it and knew it would provide my coping mechanism for that day. I claimed that verse and put my name in it. I had the victory, even though it looked like I was defeated.

God... oh what an awesome God He is. He kept me hidden until a time such as this to reveal His Glory. With Him, we are on a winning team. How can we fail? Joy will come and it is coming soon. Are you getting ready to be blessed? Well, hang on — it's coming! So be encouraged, woman of God. Be encouraged. You are going to make it!

Do not let the wall build back up again. It is time to pray, especially if you are right on the verge of getting your divorce papers. Stop right now. I want to help you get rid of everything that is keeping you from moving on. It is going to take some time alone with just you and God, the same God who helped me and is willing to help you right where you are.

To know for sure if you have forgiven your ex-husband, ask yourself:

Are you still hurting?

Does your heart break when you start talking about what happened?

If you answered yes to one of these questions, there may be some lingering un-forgiveness. Slowly get rid of it by acknowledging that you are hurting. Ask God for the gift of forgiveness to come into your heart and wash it away. Write it down and look at it one last time, then let it go. Tear it up, and then throw it away. Now God has it in His hands. You are no longer protecting yourself and God is in control.

DO NOT FAINT

PLEASE whatever you do, do not give up and do not faint. All I kept hearing from others was, "It is going to be all right." I tried to hide the hurt, but deep down I was in pain and the words from well-meaning friends wasn't enough. My circumstances kept reminding me that I had nothing — no money and no way out.

I also knew that was a lie from the pits of hell. Still, I got so weak once I almost fell out. I did not tell anyone except my 12-year-old granddaughter as I drove her to school. My granddaughter is very mature and knows how to pray. Bless her heart; she prayed a sweet and honest prayer that made me feel better.

At times, you may get tired and feel faint. At those times you are making an imprint in the enemy's camp. The devil can sense your weakness and loves nothing more than to torture weak souls. But you will overcome because you are a winner on a winning team. God is your source of strength, so draw from that. Stop and fill up on the living water that will enable you to continue. Your strength must come from God. Put all your expectations in Him. He is able to deliver you, and no one else can.

Run the race with power and perseverance. Make up your mind that you are not going to quit, and that you are going to make it. That's one thing that I held on to until the end. I knew I was going to make it, and no one could take that away from me. Once I kept that as my focus, the feelings of fainting passed me by. I could rise up like an eagle and keep on flying.

You may get most of your attacks during this period. You may hear lies like this:

You are crazy.

Why don't you just give it all up?

Look how old you are.

You do not see anything yet.

You are just a dreamer.

These tactics have all been used before in the Bible. Just put yourself in there. We are all somewhere on those pages. If there was ever a time to faint, this would be it — but you are in good company. Read about the men and women in the Bible who were faced with seemingly insurmountable odds. See? You aren't the only one. We have all gotten our equal share of attacks. However, you will learn from each one, and keep yourself girded up at all times. Never take off your armor when the fainting comes. Sleep with it on and wake up with it on. You are going to have to pray your way out of this.

Determine that you are not going to stay where you are. Don't you realize that you have an army of angels on your side? Do not be afraid, for God is with you! Keep pacing yourself. In the race to win there are no seats on the side lines. Just slow down when you need to, but do not stop.

You can do it.

Do not faint, for your season is coming. Do not use your mouth to cancel out your breakthrough. When the only one you have to talk to is your child, do not tell them everything that went wrong in your marriage. There is only so much they can take. It may seem like they are doing fine, but when you overload them with stuff you cannot deal with, how can you expect them to deal with it? What usually happens is that they end up being put in the middle and it forces them to take sides. You do not want to put your children through this, as it makes the children angry not at just your ex-husband, but at you, as well.

Do not try to make them patriots in your personal battle. Do not draft them into a marital war. Allow them to be children and encourage them to love both their parents. Make sure your children are respecting you and your ex-husband. Remind them that you are the parent (and act like one). You should not want to hurt your ex-husband through your children, even though it may seem he has no problem hurting you. Do not do evil, for with evil no one wins in this case. God still loves both of you.

It bears repeating. Please avoid the mistake of injecting your children in to grown up business. They have enough to handle. Besides, this is their father or grandfather you are talking about. Do not say negative things about him to anyone. The enemy is listening to every word and waiting to use those words to blackmail you. Family members may feel protective of you and may say bad things about your ex-husband... and then you find out later that they have become best of friends. So don't agree with them. Stop them right away. In a nice way say, "I don't want to talk about it." They will get the message and realize they can't go there with you.

There is only so much of this you can take, so stay away from the negative talk. If you cannot say anything good, then do not say anything at all.

Do not faint. The enemy would love to see you give up. He can only hinder, but not defeat you. Work overtime and encourage yourself. Repeat confessions from the Bible, make copies and put them under your pillow. Watch your diet very carefully if you are feeling faint in your spirit. You may feel weak and vulnerable in the natural, so make sure you drink lots of water and eat fruits and vegetables. Most importantly, do not forget to eat your spiritual food — the word of God. It will fortify you as the enemy throws everything he has at you during this time. Remember, that is all the devil has (accusations) and he is on his last leg.

I recall getting nightmares about my ex-husband and never any good dreams. I took more Tylenol pills than I can count to get rid of the headaches and stiff shoulders. I also made the mistake of talking to my ex-husband on the phone during a vulnerable time, and that bothered me for days. He had nothing good to say. I made things worse by trying to explain myself, which was not necessary. God is our vindicator. If you have done nothing wrong, do not look for man to vindicate you, because he cannot and most likely will not. Do not waste any time trying to explain your heart and circumstances to anyone. People are going to have their own opinions anyway.

When the fainting stops, it becomes joy in the morning. So start putting your praise on. Start thanking God that He has something better in store for you. Do not give up, do not cave in, and do not quit.

Do not faint.

Once in the spirit I felt myself in an emergency room. I was lying on a table and felt people around me. Someone was sitting at the foot of my bed. I was in a coma but could hear people around me talking to one another. I had fainted and they were all trying to bring me back. I just knew it had to be Jesus setting at the foot of my bed, caring for me. It seemed I was like this for several days. But for some reason I did not feel alone. I am not going to say that it is going to be all good all the time. Just know you won't be like this forever, and that Jesus knows your sorrows. As you began to come out of it, do not forget to say, "Thank you, Jesus." Jesus will never let us stay in limbo, shackled to a miserable existence. He is like a parent coming to the rescue. He will save his children and proved it on the cross. What more evidence do we need to convince us of His tremendous love? You are completely safe and totally wise to trust your savior.

At times I felt as if I was suffocating and was nauseated in my stomach. I do not know where this came from, but I did not think I was going to make it. All news was bad news. I did not dare let myself get happy for any length of time. Out of the four seasons, summer, winter, spring and fall, I was stuck in the winter. Keep your coat on until you are hot and on fire for the Lord. God already knows the outcome, and if you are still longing for Him,

He may give you a glimpse of you making it. I used this mental picture of God helping me succeed every time I would start to feel faint. Yes, I visualized the success He had in store for me. I also saw a rainbow over a winding highway and a large ocean of water with me reaching for the other side. That image meant that I reached the shore.

I had my granddaughter draw a pictures of a peaceful images of a woman who made it through the difficult storms in her life. Ask God to draw a picture upon your heart of your future. All you need is a glimpse — just enough for the fainting to quit. Just a little encouragement to calm your spirit down. You have been like this for so long that a small glimpse is better than nothing. Start to expect that God will answer you. Ask in confidence. Every time I did so, calmness would come over me. I would start to smile and say, "Thank you Jesus, I made it."

I am honored that God used these mental images to bless me. It was always a privilege to love Him, and I did not think I could ever love Him enough. The confidence I built up inside overwhelmed me. It is the reason why I could not quit or give up. I was determined to see it to the end and believed in the assurances of the one who had meant so much to me in the past, present and future. Please listen to me do not give up. You are worth something, and do not let anyone tell you that you are nothing. I was told this so often that started believing it myself, until I began listening to God. How foolish to drink of man's poison when we can sip at God's refreshing word.

You are everything in Christ Jesus, and He will come to your rescue in some form or fashion. When I felt downtrodden, as if one boot after the other had stomped all over me, it was then that God sent my children to help me get out from under the mess. Likewise, you do not have to stay down on the floor. You will be helped back up. I should know, because I got to the point where I simply could not take it anymore. My last prayer in my home was, "Lord, please take me out of this." As I prayed this for the second time, my prayers were answered. My life was spared and thank God, I got out. I got out!

You can get out too! It is not too late for you. If you can look up, you can get out of an abusive situation. Get the positive picture and keep it in front of you. Remember that God can certainly pull you out of any crisis. Stand on the promises He made. Claim them! You are the head and not the tail. You are above and not beneath. Just know that God is with you through it all. Cry out to Him and listen for instructions. You cannot be separated from His love because He absolutely will not allow it. Stay strong through this—do not give up. Listen to what God is saying to you.

If you have gotten this far, you might as well go on. Keep pushing, for your break through is on the other side. This is why you have been feeling faint — the devil is kicking and screaming, because he knows you have your hand on the prize. He knows you can feel it and almost see it... because it is yours. So do not let it slip away. Your joy will come. Mine certainly did, because I know that God loves me and has a plan for my life.

The ultimate plan for me, personally, was to write about the hearts of hurting women. God gave me a heart to press on and let the life of God shine through me to comfort you. God commissioned me to do this years ago, right after I received Him as my personal Lord and Savior. I knew why I was born.

You have a mission, as well. It may be to write your own book, start a business, minister to a hurting world, be an example to the lost, or just to teach the devil a lesson. God's continues His plan in each of us, with the goal to bring others to Christ. God had saved me for Himself. I did not think I was better than anyone else, but I knew I was different, just as you are different. We are not clones. We are individually and wonderfully made for a purpose. We each have gifts and talents that we should not waste, but rather uncover and nurture and use for God's glory.

Remembering back one day, the spirit of God fell very heavily on me. I was getting ready to visit a family member to pray for them. God told me about my future. In my future was a huge audience of people whose lives had been touched in some way and somehow by my existence. The spirit of God revealed just what I could handle at the time. In my spirit, I felt this was just the tip of the iceberg. However, I took what the Spirit of God had revealed and kept it at the back of my mind. I did not know what else to do with this great revelation. At the time I, did not think I was equipped to be used like that.

Likewise, you have your own great commission. You may already know what it is, or you may be learning as you go. Regardless, keep your heart and mind wide open to receive your instructions. God can and will use you in a remarkable way. You are either a blessing, or a blessing about to happen, and someone, somewhere will be profoundly touched because you are alive, and you have survived, and you have grown in wisdom. You're suffering and trials have made you a prime instrument for the Kingdom. Though you may be walking through fire, just know that you will come out bronzed and ready for your life's mission.

I often think about my life and how I got to this point. As a child I felt I was "the accident" that was not supposed to happen. My mother thought she had finished having all her children (nine by then), most of whom were grown when I came along. It surprised her, and she thought she was going through menopause. Here comes the 10th child born to parents who are 41 and 42 years old.

I stayed hidden in the background, not on purpose, but it just happened that way. When my siblings introduced me as their sister, people would say, "You're what? I never knew about you." People thought I was my parent's grandchild. My mother would say, "No that is my baby, the last pea in the dish." In the town I grew up in, if my last name was not Ankum, no one would have cared about me. All the way through school that name quickly passed through my little town then slowly stopped at me. Before the teachers ever met me, they accepted me because of my name. Somehow, I felt I might have disappointed them because everyone seemed too have lived up to the name and fit the profile... except for me.

I was not popular, smart or pretty. Women of God, we were all little girls at one time. Whatever affected you growing up is also connected to who you are today. I found out I was somebody, finally, because I am a child of God — not because of who I was connected to on the family tree. Christ chose to be a nobody and became a savior. When you are connected to Christ, it means you are the daughter of the most high God. You are not a dirty little rag. Christ lives inside of you. When you say negative things about yourself, how do you think that makes God feel? You are talking about His child. Never, ever, insult God's child (meaning you).

Please remember the only name you will ever need to remember is Jesus. This name has power everywhere you go. Therefore, when you feel like you are going to faint call on that name. Shout JESUS! I tried it, and it works.

JOY COMES IN THE MORNING

GRAB hold of the joy that comes, and learn to enjoy it. You may have forgotten what it feels like to be happy. So take advantage of it. God wants to see us enjoy ourselves and be happy. He has given us joy to refresh us and make us stronger.

You cannot blame God if you are not having fun. If it's something that you have neglected doing, whose fault is it? I should know, for I am one of those odd people who had to figure out how to have fun. It didn't come naturally and was something I learned, thanks to my family.

While writing this book, God gave me brief opportunities to take breaks. But when I had gotten behind two chapters, well, I soon learned I was operating outside of His will. So you might have to pass up the lengthy vacations and be satisfied with short breaks. You may have to discern the difference between "smelling the roses" and goofing off. Believe me, when I got lazy in my writing, God took me to task.

At this point in my post-divorce journey, my new jobs were to 1.) Write and 2.) Assist with my grandchildren, who really needed me. My daughter was a single mother of four children and was not getting any child support. My son was in the military with a wife and three children.

I took on these assignments as if they were paying jobs and worked unto the Lord... taking into consideration my fallible human nature. First and foremost, my most important "job" was helping my family. That took precedence over anything else. Let me make this clear: helping to raise my grandchildren was a blessing, not a chore, and I was blessed through every minute of it. As for my family, I did not get in their way, and by no means did I take over. I did what I was supposed to do and they appreciated me as much as I appreciated them. Neither of my children had any problems when it came to handling the financial obligations. They knew the God whom I trusted would not let us down.

Therefore, with His help, we got through it. And my goodness, what a blessing my family was to me during this time. They, literally, taught me to have fun. About six months after my divorce, joy came in the morning. Everything began to look different and smell different. I started to dance with my grandchildren. For two days in a row, I had favor. That was a profoundly new experience for me. I enjoyed it so much that I had a new challenge — I had to strike a balance between writing, raising grandchildren, and goofing off. Because everybody was so happy, and because I sensed such family harmony, I did not want to ever leave my "break room." But I knew I could not stay, because I had homework to do — a book to write.

Writing this book really has been a job — no different than a job you may have. It was my calling, but in no way am I suggesting that you quit your job to pursue a dream. So please do not do that. My opportunity was different, because I believe this book had to be written and I witnessed how God placed me within my family to make is possible. Likewise, you can do whatever God is telling you to do, and He has already placed it inside of you. I always knew that this book was a ministry to be written for you, and not me, and that is why God required me to carry on and take it seriously.

And like any worker, sometimes I veered off course. There were days I would continue to dibble and dabble in anything that would take me away from the writing. But God knows me very well. He knew if I had gotten a job outside the home, this book would probably still be on the back burner. People have done this for years, taking outside jobs and still writing books. However, that was not what God wanted me to do. He knows me too well and placed me in a situation that helped me complete the task, even when I wasn't the most cooperative "employee."

After I got half way through, I experienced a dry spell. I know it sounds silly, but there were times when I "relapsed." I fell off the joy wagon and began to fear being happy, thinking that it was only setting me up to be sad again. I did not want to be either, so I stayed in the middle. I was still experiencing life in a new way, and was growing emotionally as a newly single woman. So my personal challenge was to grow a funny bone. I had to master the art of finding and experiencing life-changing, soul-elevating joy!

It can be very challenging retaining joy when you do not feel like it. Writing brought with it emotional ups and downs. There were times when I had no idea how I was going to finish chapter after chapter. I labored very hard, and the bottom line is I could not write this type of book without experiencing it first. I had to be intimately familiar with the journey and brutally honest about the twists and turns we women face while living through a divorce.

As I struggled with writer's block, my joy would come in brief, reluctant spurts. At times I did not want to expend much effort on being happy, for I felt it was wasting my time. Instead I wanted to get this over with (the writing) with so I could move on to something else. And then I would get stuck and found excuses to procrastinate. Frankly, I wasted time being frustrated when I could have wasted the same amount of time experiencing joy!

Thankfully, the rest of the family did not feel this way. They truly enjoyed themselves, and through them I found glimpses of joy I had never knew existed. I thank God my daughter made sure the children had their share of fun and enjoyment. I enjoyed seeing other people happy, and slowly, but surely, joined in. Honestly, I cannot say that I have conquered this completely. I think once we have been miserable for so long it is hard to recognize a good time when we see it. We have been beaten down spiritually, emotionally and physically until we do not believe it's for us. We are not use to this new life filled with joy and happiness.

Joy will come, but it is up to you to grab it. Throughout my life, I developed a bad habit — I let others choose my happiness. It was difficult for me to make decisions and stick to it, in fear of hurting or offending others. They would ask me, "What do you want to do?" I would always say, "Whatever you want to do." Now for the first time, I am learning to be happy and making my own decisions regarding what makes me happy. I'm also learning many new things about myself as an individual. When you have been a couple for so long and now find yourself going solo, you are like a newborn. There are all these new ideas and you don't know what to do with them. You can eat when you feel like it. Go where you want. You are learning how to be happy again.

Joy is a rejoicing time in the Lord. You will find peace through this joy, which allows you to relax and enjoy yourself. I compare it to when our children have been studying and do well on their report cards. As parents, we want to do something special for them. But when they don't study and don't turn in assignments on time, they get bad grades. That is not something to celebrate. Rather, it is a teachable moment. We have to encourage our young students to do better and live up to their potential. But that admonition also applies to grownups. God has high standards for us. He expects us to live up to His challenges and enjoy His blessings. Sometimes we fail in both aspects, but remember that we worship a God of second chances. There will always be a next time, and God gives us new opportunities.

He doesn't tolerate laziness or lack of effort — at least not for long. I know from personal experience that God prompts us to keep going. He wants us to stay in His will and on course. He has great things to accomplish through us, but knows our limitations. That is why He allows us to catch our breath and take occasional breaks.

You can enjoy some fun times on these breaks if you want to. So go ahead. You deserve it. Do not allow the weight of the world to be a burden on you. God recognizes a good student, one who has been studying hard and staying up late to prepare for the next day. It has not gone unnoticed; God sees all and knows all. He knows when we are working hard, and he knows when we are slacking. Take my grandson, for instance, who entered high school. About three weeks into the semester I asked him what his grades were going to be. He said he had no idea. Why? Because he knew he had not given his best effort.

Should he expect to get a break? Honestly, in this day and time you have to earn your breaks. Expect to get a break when you have done well, and start looking forward to a new day. It is your day and God made it especially for you. His expectations of us include hard work and those occasional breaks. He wants us to enjoy life while fulfilling his objectives.

Do not stand back and let opportunities pass. Grab hold, for your time is now. Once you've launched out, you cannot go back. You are in too deep now, so just do it. Sometimes you might have to be strategic as you navigate your future. For example, instead of telling your dreams to everyone, consider waiting. You do not need anyone's negative feedback to hinder you or steal your joy. I felt it was a good for me to tell a couple of people about my writing endeavors. Of course, I had to tell my children, who became great inspirations when I got stuck.

So do you think that God is not a fun God?

God is fun. He laughs and plays with us. I think He even tells us jokes in our spirit, because one day I was driving along and all the sudden I started to laugh for no reason. I laughed so hard until I cried. I love it when He makes me laugh. God knows all of us very well. He knows that at times I've struggled to relax and enjoy the moment. I am the type of person who always needs to be doing something. But I did not want to be labeled as being "too spiritual and no earthly good," so I set out to purposely have fun. Yes, I'm the type who had to force myself to have fun. But once I started playing games with my grandchildren, I enjoyed it. Now we laugh and have fun together all the time.

All this time I thought being with someone else made me happy. I never learned to be happy alone, and this is what I was missing. I liked being a wife and all of the caring, cooking, cleaning, bill paying and taking care of personal things. I liked giving him a foot and neck massage or taking a bath together. I enjoyed doing those things.

It's like I have had to be reprogrammed. I had to drop my will and let it be God's will. Start by introducing yourself to you. It goes something like this: get in front of a mirror and say, "Hi, my name is…" then go from there. Get to know you. Then see yourself the way God sees you, not the way people see you. God loves you just the way you are.

Start liking who you are. As you move forward, this is the perfect time to enjoy alone time. It doesn't take other people to make you happy. If that person leaves you, where is your happiness? I love being around my grandchildren. I am very happy and content when I am with them, but I do not revolve my life around them. They will have lives of their own one day. I don't lean on them and I don't want them to lean on me, for it would not be good for either of us. I strive to teach them independence and to stand their own ground when things are not going right. I want them to have the tools to stand for what is right.

It is not a good idea to keep replacing your mate. After all, your children are watching. Do not get involved in one relationship after the other. Take the time to find out who you are first, but don't entangle someone else in your web of confusion. You deserve a worthy male — one that God has prepared for you. How can a man say he knows who he is when he has never even bought underwear for himself? If he has always depended on someone else to do it, and you think that's cute, then you are heading for a disastrous relationship. Does this sound like an independent person and appropriate partner? Is it someone who has spent time developing a healthy foundation? I was a people pleaser and it kept me from looking at who I really was. It also kept me from seeking out — and expecting — the best in a mate.

There is no other way to say it, except to say that you have to get your joy back. The devil does not have to steal it when you hand it over to him. So many of us need direction on how to make ourselves happy. You have a voice, so use it. If you don't know where it is, go find it. Do what I did and write about it.

I let things go on for so long by saying, "It's okay," and, "Whatever." I hid behind my true feelings in fear of upsetting the other person. But when you say nothing, you just give permission for the other person to use you.

I dare you to stand up and say who you really are. It only takes a few words. Try it. No doubt, you understand what no means. Start respecting yourself by not letting people mistake your kindness for weakness, and do not let anyone walk over you. You are not a door mat. You have the right to say no, so don't feel guilty. It releases you to feel the joy you have been lacking.

You want your joy back, right? Well then start saying something. Do not let anyone take you for granted or manipulate you. Let your NO mean NO, and stand firm on it. The first few words you say to someone indicates the kind of person you are. Speak with confidence and let your voice be heard. You don't have to get all spiritual; for they will know instinctively that you are a child of God. Behind you is a generation of women who have freely given away the words that God has placed inside of them. We know it wasn't particularly easy for these women to be heard, for women in general, past and present, have often been silenced or ignored or minimalized. We know in order to have complete joy we need each other's help.

Dear Lord,

Lord, we want what belongs to us — our joy, our voice. We claim victory now and rejoice in the knowledge of knowing you won't hold anything good from us. Forgive us for giving the enemy a place in our lives, and thank you for restoring joy and a voice to be heard. In Jesus' name, amen.

I stand in agreement with every woman who has prayed this prayer. Watch what God will do. Step out when He tells you to and open your mouth. Your mouth is a weapon to use for good or bad. You can call things into existence with your mouth just like God did in the beginning when He said in Genesis 1-3, "And God said, 'Let there be light.'" Do you realize how God is going to use you? Get ready to be blessed. You cannot be stopped now. Say, "It's too late, devil, you should have got me when you had a chance!" Start getting violent in your prayer life. Do not let the devil keep taking from you. Know that through all of this you are still going to make it. Reach out and claim your joy!

Our life can be compared to an onion. God peels away one layer at a time, if we let Him. You have made the first step, and there is nothing wrong with you. Just because circumstances happened, do not be so hard on yourself. We all make mistakes. It happens. We are not perfect. Do not dwell on the past, and go beyond it. Leave it alone and expect good things. It is time to take a break and have fun. Where should you start?

Put the book down and do something. Laugh and enjoy yourself — try it. The book will still be there when you come back.

Welcome back. You are a new person now, someone you just met for the first time. You are a beautiful person, a fun person and a person with a voice. Once you have taken this stand, you will never be the same. People will look at you as if they are seeing you for the first time, and they are. You have finally gotten their attention, and they see the Christ in you. Your light is shining and everyone notices. You have a light that the enemy tried to put out, but you passed that challenge because you didn't give up.

There are a lot of people depending on you. Do it for them, but most of all do it for you. Every woman counts. Everything we go through concerns God and it should concern you. Encourage someone today and let them know that they are going to make it, and that joy will come.

CHAPTER FIVE

FINDING YOUR PLACE

I have always had a problem trying to fit in. I was too spiritual to fit into the world, and was not political enough to be around church people. So where was I supposed to be? I started searching the Bible, then remembered that Jesus did not fit in either. Therefore, I made my mind up that I wanted to be just like Him.

When you want to know where your place is, ask God. He knows everything. He knows where you are supposed to go to church. He knows how to heal your heart when it is breaking. He knows how to put all the pieces back together again, if you allow Him. At times people may reject you, especially if you made up your mind that you are going to make it. There are people who hope you don't make it, and will get pleasure when you fail. Don't let these poisonous people discourage you.

You will never find your place if you stay where you are. Do not get comfortable, and remember that there are four seasons. You must go through them all.

After my divorce I got rid of all the little constant reminders, like some pictures we had taken together on vacation. I only saved a few for my children to keep in their albums. After about nine months, I forgot what he looked like. There were no more hurt feelings left in me to remind me, and no more personal items or pictures to jog my memory. Your children will move on and love both of you. I am very thankful that they did not hold any grudges against either of us. Do not teach your children to have a hateful heart. Release them, so the toxicity won't get passed on to their children. Teach them to love their father or grandfather.

My children realized there was something different about me, for I was definitely not like the other parents. I remember being quiet and never having much to say. I often just stood back. Early in our marriage, we went out with a few couples. One couple in particular would pull out a deck of cards whenever we went to visit them. I was the only one who didn't know how to play. They all had their laughs while trying to teach me. I felt so out of place when it came time to choose partners. No one wanted to lose the game, and by choosing me they were sure to lose. I tried to pretend I was enjoying myself, but I wasn't. I became very bored.

My next task of fitting in was going to nightclubs with other couples. I would get sleepy just setting there. I could not dance like the rest of them. They tried teaching me. Fast dancing was a little difficult, so I stuck with slow dancing. By midnight, I would be sleepy and ready for bed. But my party friends were far from ready to go home. These people partied from Thursday night until Sunday evening. I got no pleasure in that lifestyle.

Nevertheless, the other couples to this day still like a good party. Some have even joined a church, but continue with the same-o, same-o. When I was growing up, there was not any difference when you joined a church. Most people continued to curse, cheat in their marriage, go to clubs, and gamble. I prayed after I was saved and asked the Lord do not let me be a fake Christian. I prayed, "Let my love for you be pure and real." I even rejected the old music I used to listen to, and my life changed very quickly.

I often wondered why I did not end up like those friends. It seemed normal to be married and have someone else "on the side," even for pastors. Back then, there was no one who made it through the 12th grade without getting pregnant. Being a virgin was out of the question. My mother had six girls, and all six became pregnant before graduation. No matter who you were, you fit into the norm. Even for me, a quiet girl who didn't go anywhere, I still ended up pregnant. However, I was not wild like most girls. The boy that I ended up liking was very popular and one of the most handsome around school.

My first relationship started in the 9th grade. That's when I met my first boyfriend. I remember him following me home from a late night baseball game at the neighborhood park. I tried to play hard to get for a minute, but he won me over. Besides winning me over, he also won two other girls at the same time. My town was so small; there were two women to one man. This really bothered me, and it was very stressful trying to keep up with my "boyfriend" and all the other girls he went out with.

After I got pregnant I found out he also had two of his other girlfriends pregnant, as well. He turned his back on me and my daughter without any child support. Therefore, I took the rejection and then met another man, who not only wanted to marry me, but wanted to become a father to my daughter. I really wanted my daughter's father to want the two of us, but he didn't, so I accepted another man's hand in marriage with the feeling of failure looming before me.

Along with my bondage and the stuff he brought to our marriage, we were off to a bad start. I never knew he was engaged to someone else, but left her and married me instead. It didn't end there. The women whom he was engaged lived in another state, but somehow found him and made our first year of marriage miserable. She became a "fatal attraction" type of character and was out to get us both.

Please, women, don't run to another man after you have just been rejected. Take time to know one another. Talk and ask a lot questions. Find out about his past relationships and do your research.

So here were two wounded people, and both of us knew very little about God. We were both out of place and out of order, and had nothing in common. Shortly after my marriage I got pregnant with our first child together. I knew then that my place was to be the best mother and wife possible, so that is what I set out to do. I am not trying to say I was Miss Goody Two Shoes all the time, because I wasn't. But I did try. Oh, how I tried!

As I continued to find my place, I was getting desperate to know why I was on this earth. So I had a talk with my older brothers and sisters. I spoke with pastors and started reading self-help books. I wrote down things that would come to mind about my life, until one day I was reading the Bible. I suddenly stopped and out of nowhere I decided to ask, "God, who am I and why am I here?" I had so many more questions for God.

The answer? This is what spoke to my heart: God made me for Himself. My name, L U C I L L E, means

Loved

Unique

Compassionate

Intelligent

Loyal

Lasting

Excellent

It seems as though I had waited a lifetime to finally find this out. It was as if this wide door of knowledge opened before me. Information started to pour in. Then I realized God had hidden me for this special moment. He knew I would come to Him, so He was ready to answer all my questions. The person you are looking for lies deep within you, waiting to come out. I wanted to explore the depth of my soul. Once I tapped into who I was, I found a spiritual connection between me and God.

As you find your place, start to challenge yourself. Do not get stale doing the same thing. Ask God, "What else?" There has got to be more to life than being a wife and mother. There is something big on the inside of you waiting to burst out. Women, do not settle. Launch out. What do you have to lose?

I often thought of marriage as this perfect little relationship with a white picket fence, living happily ever after, like in a fairy tale. No one could ever see this picture except me. I went into marriage thinking it was supposed to last until death do us part. I never thought it could be that hard. When we used to play house as a child, we always portrayed a happy family. Not until my 40th birthday did I realize and understand that I was not playing house anymore. This was real. I needed to find a place where I belonged.

Most of us are looking for a real love. That kind of love can only come from God. I became so desperate, I remember saying softly, "Please God, help me." I think the moment God heard that, it touched His heart. After I said it, I began to see great victory everywhere I turned. I believe what I was searching for found me. Shortly after the passing of my mother, I heard these words dropped in my spirit: "I love you." Right away it went straight through me. I jumped up with surprise and shouted out, "He loves me, He loves me, God loves me!"

I was overwhelmed and nothing else mattered, because I knew God loved me. Why would a God love someone like me, undeserving as I was? I knew without a doubt that those words spoken to me, "I love you," came straight from God. Jesus has the same voice open to you today. He is saying it to those women who don't think they are worth much. Can you hear Him calling you, saying, "Daughter I love you." If you are wondering where that soft gentle voice comes from, it is from Jesus — His heart to yours.

Women of God, He knows who you are. He wants you to locate yourself. God has given me a heart for you. Through this book we are connected. We are sisters. Don't you dare give up. It might not seem like it now, but believe me; you are going to make it. I did, and so will you. It will take more than what you are going through now to stop you. Do the right thing and God will do right by you.

At one point, I found myself settling down and writing a book that identified with me today. Everyone has a story to tell, because we have all gone through something. I know that I am not the only one this memoir is for. It's for you, as well. You cannot hide what you have been going through from anyone except yourself. You certainly can't hide it from God.

And speaking of God, he sees the victories and failures in all of us. Say you get up on Sunday, prepare yourself to teach Sunday school, and there you see the child whose mother has been sleeping with your husband. Just because you are a pastor's wife does not mean you are not going through stuff. Why make it pretty because he is a pastor of a church? When he fails, it will affect many people. He has already affected many people by having the affair in the first place. Where do you think I got this material? Yes, this once happened in my church. God can see you sweeping it under the rug and acting as if it didn't happen.

This is not God's best for you. Get to a place where God sees you. Remember that you are made in His image. You have a Father who loves you. You have the kind of love that is active, not passive. This kind of love will go to bat for you, if you allow it to. Listen to the next passage very carefully:

Once there was a woman who was diagnosed with an illness, so the entire church decided to pray for her healing. Prayers all over the Church went up for this woman. In the midst of it, the woman spoke up and said, "But I don't want to be healed. I want to die." Is this what you want, women of God? Is your life better off dead?

Please get help at once. Call on the only one who is able to help you. Unless you face it, you will never find your place in the world. Non-Christians may call us crazy, but you and I both know better. Do you realize all this time God was trying to teach you something? Do not let anyone tell you that God does not love you. I used to believe everything that someone told me. I was just like a little child believing in Santa Claus. With great anticipation my eyes lit up with excitement, and I would say, "For real?"

Anyone could tell me anything and I would believe it. How gullible is that? Nevertheless, I promise you that deep down inside me I never ever believed that God did not love me. I remember preparing for the coming of 2000. We all had supplies to pick up, an entire list of emergency items we needed like candles, matches, canned food, water, etc. just in case the world was coming to an end. I did just like the list instructed. Got all the stuff... and we all know nothing happened when the clock struck midnight and the year 2000 dawned upon us.

At times I felt I was a follower and not a leader. Followers don't need to say anything, because they don't have a voice. Even the few times I had the opportunity to be a leader, I had doubts because I had gotten so stressed out and didn't believe in my own abilities. In the leadership role that I had for a short time, there was no such thing as a mistake. Mistakes were just not tolerated even while you were trying to find yourself.

But when you find your place, you have just unlocked the miracles that are inside of you. Do not ever go back to being a silent partner in a relationship. Speak up, because you are somebody. Take time and find out where you belong. It took a lot of hard work to get you this far — do not give it up over a lie.

Somewhere deep within God's heart is a place just for you, so step up to the plate and take your position. You are at bat now. It is up to you how far you want to go in life.

TIME SPENT IN PRAYER

I remember finding time to do everything else except pray. I move around a lot during the day. I might notice the floor needs mopping, furniture needs dusting, and it seemed like any little thing got in my way when it came to spending time with God.

Even though I loved spending time in His presence (praying is one of my favorite things to do), instead I made myself vulnerable to the distractions around me. Occasionally, if a creditor called it got me off focus and I let it bother me for a while. I could not just let that go. On top of that, I started to take it personally. Then it took me two days to build up my prayer life again. But people just kept messing with me. Instead of arming myself with prayer, I allowed myself to be distracted.

I like it when I am able to wake up at 5:00 am to pray. That way, if I get busy throughout the day at least I will have had that time in. This is a very important event in your life — prayer time. Without a doubt, one thing you are going to need for the duration of your life is God. Praying is one sure way to reach Him. I love hearing testimonies of people who spend hours in prayer. They all seem so vibrant and energetic. Whenever I would do this, I felt the same way. However, sometimes it could be hard to get in that prayer time. There were many distractions in my home to overcome, and I am happy to share a few tips to help you stay focused as you enter into your place of prayer:

I had a family meeting with my children and grandchildren and explained to them how important this was to me. And I asked for their help. I made them feel that not only would I benefit, but it would also teach them how to be considerate and respect others. Talk to your children and they will understand.

Unexpected phone calls? Let the answering machine pick up your messages. Church committees? If you serve on any kind of a prayer group, let your partners know that you need coverage between certain hours. In fact, many times I hear people say they are busy with intercessory prayer, choir and other groups. They get themselves involved with every ministry and do not take time to have private sessions with God.

We wear so many hats, and sometimes it is hard to keep up. The devil tries to over-involve you in many things so that you will take your eyes off God. I admit I used to be in a lot of ministries, such as intercessory, praise and worship, and a Sunday school teacher. I was going somewhere every night. Now I know that is not what God wants for me during this season. In fact, God will not let me get too involved anymore and my ministry is very limited.

You see, I want to spend as much personal time with my Father God as possible. I don't want to ever be found being too busy for Him. I realize a time may come when my calendar is full again, but I will be selective. Please do not get tied down with the weight of the world. Even though you are busy in the Church, the devil will still try to ease in. Put first things first.

God is always first. Seek and aim at God's way first. Allow God to order your steps, for He will not direct you wrong. Time spent in prayer will always be a benefit. Prayer is necessary, as it helps build you up so you can be strong and able to face anything. Position yourself to be blessed. God will honor you.

Once I made up in my mind that I wanted to touch the heart of God, I was willing to do whatever it took. I sincerely loved God with all my heart and want Him in every way and any way I could get Him. I read in Proverbs that those who search for Him shall surely find Him. So I was determined to go on a search to find God — or a "journey" — as I have learned to call it. Along the way, I went to various levels: Ask and it shall be given, Seek and ye shall find, Knock and it shall be open. All I had to do at each level was simple. I got pretty much everything I prayed for every time.

1.) Ask for: I started my in home care business with 24-hour clients. This was easy for God, a piece of cake! I got it, no problem.

2.) Seek and ye shall find: I had been looking for someone to talk to about my Christian walk. I met a young Chaplin who just started her internship and was new to the area. She became my counselor for two years.

3.) Knock and it shall be open: I wanted to know about my spiritual gifts and discovered I am an intercessor. I had the opportunity to go to a three-day conference on spiritual warfare with fellow intercessors from all over the world. Praying was easy and fun. Every time I prayed, I got answers. When I prayed for other people, God moved in their lives, as well.

After a while, I got so involved in the things I prayed for, that I did not want to stop. Your prayer time sets a "presence of God" atmosphere everywhere you go, and it affects everything you do. This is a powerful weapon, so use it for every area of your life. For instance, it is a good idea during weekly service to pray for Sunday service, because many people only go to Church on Sundays. Before you leave a church, start to pray for your Pastor. Ask God for divine direction.

Your prayer time is a direct connection to God. You speak and God speaks. If you are the only one talking, that is not good communication, so wait on God to response back. If you do not get anything back, just remember the last thing you heard from Him. Chances are, He is still saying to stand on that. Do not pretend that you do not understand that God is telling you to pray for your ex-husband. If God said it, you had better do it.

Whenever you step out to do anything for God, the enemy will try to attack you. That is his job: to hinder and distract you. There was an attack on my prayer life because I like to pray and I experienced no problems while I was in prayer. Therefore, this was my Goliath over which I needed victory. In this case, it required fasting. Whatever prayers you are able to do, use them and fast. As I prepared to do a fast, I usually got everything ready first. Here are the weapons I used: Bible confession (God's word, God's promises), olive oil (anointing), wine and crackers (communion), prayer list, praise and worship music, paper and pencil, reading glasses, spiritual tapes and videos, box of tissue.

Once I make a decision to fast, I start right away. If this is a working day for you, you may need to alter your schedule. I usually ask for a prayer partner, and we get together in person or by telephone, text or email. The two of us have the same material and start and stop at the same time. The day of the fast opens with prayer, anointing ourselves with olive oil, and singing praise and worship songs. If this is a work day, start a little early. Now continue your day in your daily routine. If you are on medication or taking vitamins, you may need to alter your fast. Some medication and vitamin intake require food, so I would never advise you not to eat. If you need to eat or drink, then do it and keep at a minimum. Continue the fast. Every hour do something on your list. The last hour do Communion and an ending prayer.

Then eat fruits or vegetables and drink water. Let this be your first meal after you come off a fast if you are doing anything over eight hours. Everybody will tell you something different when it comes to a fast. My advice is to listen to the guidance of the Holy Spirit. He is the one who guided me. The same Holy Spirit that led Jesus into the wilderness on a 40-day fast will be leading you. If you get a little weak, cry out to God to help you. If you need to talk to your prayer partner, now is a good time. Be completely honest with God do not hold anything back. If you do not get an answer, continue the next week in the same manner. Continue to fast each week until you get a release. You will get your prayer life back. If it happens again, now you know what to do. The enemy cannot rob you of this because you have a blood-brought right. This time belongs to you and God. Time spent in prayer is essential and you need it as the handle to the cup you drink.

In the middle of everything, I had to stop and spend time with God — just Him and me without this book. I was not spending enough time with God because the book was taking every extra minute. Even though God knew my heart, I still needed to get in His word and meditate into the fullness of who He is. That was necessary in order for me to keep my perspective clear. It's always God first. Do not ever lose sight of God being number one in your life. Even though writing books is my ministry, it will never take the place of God. He is the one and only. God is clear about not putting any idols before Him. That could even mean the book, the kids or whatever.

I remember when I had my business, it prevented me from attending Bible study on Wednesday nights. I remember someone asking me, "How you can know for sure if something is from God or not?" Good question. I realized that if something is taking you away from the things of God, it is not a real blessing. God will never take away from Himself. I think you need to test it and see.

PROMOTION

Promotion takes you to higher ground. Your finances will increase. You will lose longtime friendships that have become toxic. You are now starting a new branch. Get used to the good life now, for your time has come and you made it. There is nothing wrong with you, and your family is alive and enjoying the good life.

After you have gone as low as you can go, you will truly know who your friends are. Promotion should bring about change and new challenges. You are at a different level and have graduated to another faith; your promotion came from God.

Now everybody wants to be your friend. You endured and you stood, no matter what. People had written you off, but you stayed firm to the promises of God. You were talked about and laughed at, and no one gave you a second thought. Yet now your time is here. You might get some phone calls now, even though yesterday the phone never rang. Now that you have money again, you are looking good to those same people who turned their back on you. Now you can carry your own weight and are not an "embarrassment" anymore. So now it's "Let's go shopping together."

This means that God is well pleased with you. You are passing the test and it is time to celebrate. God has proven He is faithful. This is a new day, so now remember where you came from. Thank God you did not end up in poverty like everyone thought. You are on top. Do not forget to say thank you. Where would you be without the Lord on your side? You are recovering all that the devil stole from you and seven times more. Do not take your armor off; you are going to need it, and more. There will be new demons waiting, and possibly old demons that are surprised you made it this far. You missed all the darts and came out smelling like a rose.

This is the day that God has made for you. Enjoy it and look forward to moving on. You are in the cycle and do not have time anymore for anyone who is "playing church." You are on a mission and want to hear God say on the Day of Judgment, "Well done." As I think back to who I was and compare it to the new person I am now since my divorce, I would never put up with the foolishness I did back then. Along with the promotion comes maturity. No longer will you require milk. You will know when the word is being watered down or sugar-coated, and your spirit will check you. You are able to feed on meat now. You do not easily get offended like you used to.

Things that I use to let go unchecked, I fight for now. I have a voice. For example, my insurance company tried to rip me off. Even though it was an error, they would not give me my $150.00 back. The company refused to refund what belonged to me, so I had to take it to another level. I targeted the person in charge. After writing a letter and explaining what happened, I finally got my money. This did not have to happen, and any other time I would have said, "Forget about it." That is what they expect us to do — just forget about it. But not this time. I stood and fought for it.

Just remember to use wisdom and allow God to use you. I let my home, my business, and my marriage all go without fighting for it. At first I started to, but instead I ended up paying money to lawyers to do nothing. That is when I got so much relief from Psalm 37. God is the only one who can promote you. Make sure all your ducks are in a row. Represent excellence everywhere you go, and in everything you do, do it unto the Lord. I often tell my grandchildren, "When doing chores around the house, do it unto the Lord."

Ask yourself this question: WWJD (What Would Jesus Do)? My background prepared me for a ministry of excellence. If I had a job cleaning the toilet, then I would thoroughly clean the toilet and do a little extra. Keep this in the back of your mind: would this be acceptable to God? Use this state of mind in everything you do in life.

At one time I lived in a rented house with a large yard. I don't know why, but I didn't care about the yard. I let weeds grow instead of doing my best to make sure it looked excellent. I remember thinking, "Just wait until I get my own house with my own big yard." I planned to do much more on my "own" property, going the extra mile to make it look just right. Suddenly I got this check in my spirit. Now, just how was I going to do all that with a bigger yard... especially when I was neglecting the yard I already had? I should have been more interested in doing the best right at that level. First, I needed to prove myself where I was before I could be trusted to go further.

We tend to look every place but the right place, which in my case was right in front of my own yard. God will promote you when it is time. I like to garden, so I will use another gardening example. My garden is like my life. I spend time in my garden every day. I look at the picture of the vegetable or fruit. I start to prepare. My goal is for my seeds to look exactly like the seeds on the package. I prepared myself well and attended gardening classes, then bought books to help me relearn some things. These were all the tools I needed. Now I was ready. Whatever I am willing to grow, I invest time in it. Same with our spiritual walk with God... we want it to grow and mature to get to the next level.

See yourself the way God sees you. We are his children, so of course He wants the best for us. How do you want to see your children? Prosperous? In good health? Happy and growing in the things of God?

Is God any different? He wants what we want. What are you doing to prepare yourself to grow spiritually? What are you ready for? Every day in your garden is the precious time you spend with God. Look at this as a "word picture" — studying His word is like being in His garden. Now you are ready to plant the word and tell someone the good news. Select the dirt. The location is where you are right now; your boundaries.

We are all gardens waiting for something to be planted, and the way you plant your garden determines what you will grow. If you plant strife, it will yield anger. If you plant friendships, it will yield friends. Find out what the root is of what you have planted. You will reap what you sow—good or bad. Anything you plant will go to the next generation, so pull the root out of things you want "unplanted."

You have just been promoted. Thank God, you passed.

In the 3rd grade, I was passed "on condition" and didn't find out what that meant until I became an adult. Passed on condition means you barely made it. The condition means you may need to go to summer school or a summer home study. Regardless, some extra studying will be required. The teacher may have liked you and perhaps you had excellent behavior, but otherwise you were just not getting it. Now when God conditions you, He only wants you to trust Him. He is saying, "I will do this (the condition) if you will just trust me. I will do what I said if you would just trust me."

Can you say today that you trust Him with your hurt feelings, or trust Him with your finances? In the natural, we get a written slip with our grades, and at the bottom it says: "Promoted: passed or failed." Your Heavenly report card will read: "Promoted: passed to the next grade."

DOING THE RIGHT THING

I decided early on that I could not (refused to) live in strife with my ex-husband. I didn't hate him. I couldn't hate him even if I wanted to, because God would not let me. I did not want to fight anymore deciding who was right and who was wrong. So I made a decision to give up everything and suffer the consequences.

I knew my God had a plan and would not let me fail. Therefore, I said yes to his attorney and gave him everything he demanded. I left that town with a few personal belongings, and then released it all to God. I didn't want it anymore — none of it. My peace was more important, and nothing seemed important enough to lose my peace over. Besides, I knew my God would supply all my needs according to His riches in Glory in Christ Jesus. I leaned on Phil 4-19 because I had been faithful.

When you are doing the right thing and walking in Godly character, you can care less about what other people think. You need to know for yourself what is right and what is wrong, and you would be amazed that a lot of people don't know something as simple as that. Many times we learn as we go, and we learn as we grow. When you do the right thing, it releases you of any guilt or hard feelings. In the movie *The Color Purple*, Mister had treated his wife Celia very badly by hiding all the letters from her sister Nettie, which were mailed from Africa. In one letter, the sister goes on to explain how she ended up in Africa and became the Nanny to her sister's two children who were taken at birth. Mister's mistress found the letters and gave them to Celia. Celia confronted Mister and was furious at him for keeping the letters hidden away from her all these years. Angry and devastated, Celia told Mister that because he had done this terrible thing to her on purpose, he would have no peace until he did right by her, meaning "doing the right thing."

Well, Mister was convicted of his wrongdoing and set out to make it right by Celia. Finally, doing the right thing brought peace in his heart. Likewise, you cannot do the wrong thing and expect to have peace about it. God will not allow it.

Now, what happens when you are doing the right thing and nothing happens? Never look for anything to happen without first having faith in God. Do not waver back and forth. Decide to do well and continue in it every day without changing. You have to make a decision that you are going to do the right thing, no matter what. The right thing will put you on top. The supernatural will burst forth into the natural. So do not panic if you don't see it yet — it is coming. God has already worked it out.

I had a bad sore on my arm. It had gotten infected and was about the size of a quarter. In one week my entire arm was in pain. I used every kind of medicine I could think of, and even some homemade remedies I knew. I put medication on every few hours trying to draw the infection out. I saw no change day after day. Some of the medication burned and tingled, and I could feel the infection fighting back as the medicine penetrated into the infected area. At that moment, I realized what was happening. The healing was taken place on the inside first. Then the outside healing began — the outside skin started to peel away, just to let me know the inside healing was completed. In 10 days the dry skin fell off, and underneath was the beautiful color that was there previously. It came to full bloom.

Whatever needs to be healed, God wants to address those inner wounds first. The pain that hurt you so badly when you were a little girl may be something you haven't gotten over yet. This is where He wants to start first. He wants to heal you from the inside out completely. That is why He has set you apart from the rest of the world. It is time for your deliverance. The healing ministry is inside of you, and God wants to activate it. Let it start with you now.

A Prayer of Healing:

Dear Lord,

I have been hurt so badly. I have not told anyone except you. I want to be delivered and set free. I cannot take it anymore. I believe you can help me and I trust that you will. Help me today to put this behind me, in Jesus' name.

Now, don't get tricked back. Just leave it there; you have done the right thing. Things will start to fall off you, and you will know what happened and why. It won't bother you anymore if people don't want you in their circle. You are changing and they are not. Do not be hard on them, and remember that you were once there. You know what it is like to be in bondage.

When you step out into this way of life, you will lose friends but gain new ones. Not everyone will encourage and pray for you. In my own experience, people seemed as though they were afraid of me. I didn't get any information about anything unless it was old news. Everyone else knew and I didn't, but there were those who started to respect me and wanted to know more about my walk with the Lord. Some of them just could not figure me out.

If ever there were any hurt feelings or misunderstandings, right away I would try to make it right. This usually ended with a phone call, letter or a card of encouragement, and often an apology, if necessary. Acknowledge it and forgive them whether it is your fault or not. I was determined to clear up the confusion, because God would always convict me anyway to get it right. I couldn't just do anything or say anything like everyone else without my Father checking me. I had to learn how to talk all over again. Words like "lucky" changed to "fortunate." Words like "sickness" changed to "diagnosis." Phrases like, "I'm broke" changed to "I have more than enough." Likewise, "Love you to death" became "Love you to life." I made sure all negative words no longer came out of my mouth. I often wondered why other people could get away with talking like this, especially professed Christian people. Why didn't God check them, but always checked me? Not because he loves me more — of course not. I'm sure their time is coming, and in the meantime God was dealing with me about these issues. So I tried to stay focused on what I was supposed to do. After all, God could be dealing with them on other issues.

I am still a work in progress, and I am sure there are many other words that I say that are not correct, but I know for sure about these few. Life and death is in the power of the tongue, and I used to be a user of negative words. Maybe that is why God started in this area of my life first. I soon realized that if those words were in me, then I must have put them there. What I put in my heart was spoken from my mouth. That is what the Bible means in scriptures that are supposed to renew our mind daily. We are to think on good thoughts, and then those thoughts become a conversation, then become a dialogue between you and God or you and the devil. The Bible also teaches us how to speak to the devil. We are to denounce him in the name of Jesus.

Learn how to talk right, and you will get it right and do right. Doing the right thing means you will need Godly wisdom to get you out of the wrong choices you have made. I knew I had clearly heard from God when I prayed about what church I should attend. After six months, I finally got my answer. The church that God chose for me was one I visited previously... and hated!

Therefore, I took it upon myself to help God out by choosing another Church that I liked. Boy, was that a big mistake. I stayed in that Church for nine months and suffered dearly for not doing the right thing in the first place.

I have learned that when it comes to who teaches me, I must be sensitive to the Holy Spirit. I have learned not to react too hastily and judge another wrongfully. Do not go by what you feel, because your feelings can change, just as it changed for me. I thought I had found the best church, and certainly there wasn't anything wrong with it, but it was not for me to join — it was for me to just visit. Follow the Holy Spirit when finding a church, and even that is in God's hand. When all else fails, remember the right thing is often the first thing.

CHAPTER SIX

WALKING IN CONFIDENCE

I put my confidence in no one other than God. In Him are all the answers I need. He knows me so well, and even knows how many strands of hair are on my head. He numbered them all himself. This is confidence needed by all Christians, because so many times we slip up and put our confidence in men. Then later on we find out they let us down.

Remember, when you go with God He will never let you down. In Him you can place your trust, and you will not be disappointed. What have you put your confidence in? Is it your job, your children or yourself? Sometimes we can brag, "I did this," or "I did that." The bottom line is, you have not done anything. I know I had put a lot of confidence in my marriage, and when it ended I thought it was me who failed. Whatever you put your confidence in, other than God, will fail you. Walking in the confidence of God will bring about peace, reassurance and rest, far above what we can ever imagine.

Have you ever wondered why some people always have a happy look on their face? I met a woman like that recently. Every time I've seen her, she's had this aura of peace about her. We need to tap into this. Then again, I know people who never have the reassurance that God loves them. They are always looking down and out. They probably put their confidence in something else other than God. They became programmed and don't know how to get out of the circle. Their careers have become their source, and now they are married to the job.

One thing they won't give up is that money. It doesn't matter how unhappy they are. God has become second on their list. Chances are, even without that job that person will still be unhappy. Until you make God the primary source — not the job

— you will never have confidence.

Your job is not your source. God is. Believe that even when the job ends, God will still be there. Who do you believe? When God said, "I will never leave nor forsake you," you can believe it. Start to have confidence in God's word and watch what happens. Even go as far as putting it in your mouth every day. Every time you walk in a room, that glow starts to shine and people are happy to see you coming.

I had one of my elderly clients make up excuses to prompt me to come to her house. She would say the moment I walked in she felt calmness. Often I asked if she could call anyone else, and she insisted it had to be me. The kind of business I had gave me the opportunity to be around many elderly people. Early on, I found out that most of them were just plain lonely. My job was very demanding, to the point I start receiving calls at home. I used to tell them over and over again that I was not God and not to put me on any kind of pedestal. Nevertheless, they would try every chance they had to make me out to be something I wasn't.

I believe most of them had no relationship with God themselves, and they knew I did. Be very careful and don't let anyone put you in a place you're not supposed to be. In a kind way I directed them to God as their source — the Bread of Life. It didn't take much, just simple things like holding and rubbing their hand and telling them God loves them just to get the attention off me.

I got such confidence when I read a book on the life of Smith Wigglesworth, a man of great faith and confidence to the end. He took God at His word. He put his confidence in God. I realized that most of us do not have that. Try to find somewhere to start, perhaps with something simple, like a chair. Think about how you expect it to hold you. Take a minute and look at the chair. Now turn it around and think of the chair being God, and the confidence you have in the chair. Now put yourself in the chair (sitting down in the chair). Start to relax and know that God is in control. He is in charge of your life and He won't let you fall.

During this time in my life, there was nothing else for me. All I wanted was to move on and build a new life and continue with God in it. Let the word of God do the work for you by keeping it on your mind and in your heart and mouth at all times. Meditate in it day and night. Read Joshua 1-5. Write it down; put it on your wall, in your car and in your garage. I put it in every room of my house.

Be careful not to fall back into the evil grasp of the enemy by dangling your feelings back and forth with your husband. Stop sending him mixed signals. Sure, we allow people to have second chances, but make up your mind either way. Then leave him alone and do not make excuses to see him again. But if you feel like it is not over yet, then you may need closure. I think I would probably have considered going back if I had left before my time was up. Thankfully, my time was up as directed by God, and it helped me to realize I had done my best and that this was the end.

Women of God, you did your best. Do not ever forget that. It is time to move on, and you deserve better than to live on a memory that is dead. There is no life there anymore. I know it is hard, and I know your heart is hurting, but this confidence is medicine that will help you stand and keep you from falling. Grab it, and please do not let this pass you by. There is an anointing available to heal you from those hurt emotions.

Will you go with me now to the Father?

LET'S PRAY:

Dear God,

I am very tired right now. I have been carrying a burden that is heavy on me. The only place I want to be is at your feet. Lord, I want to be healed and leave this burden where it belongs in the first place. Help me with my unbelief. Forgive me as I now put my confidence in you, in Jesus' name.

Expect something to happen; no longer will you be the same. You have stepped into something good. Now start walking the walk and talking the talk. It does not matter that you are alone. Remember, you have God. And as your confidence grows, so will you.

Your vocabulary has increased, and now everything about you has changed. People will come from all around to try to shake you. Comments like, "You prayed about your marriage and look what happened," may strike a nerve.

So can you really trust God?

You need to be ready and know for sure what God has revealed to you. It does not matter about the temptations. Obedience is better than disobedience. In obedience, there is a great reward. My confidence began the last year of my marriage. I believed that God was preparing me for such a time as this. Walk in confidence and do not be afraid.

DO NOT BE AFRAID

DO not be afraid, because God did not give you a spirit of fear, but the power of love and a sound mind (2 Timothy 1:7). I walked in so much fear in my marriage. I would always be the one who would apologize first, because I didn't want to give him a reason to hit me. I was afraid people would not believe me when I told them, because most of the time my bruises were on the inside. Any excuse I could think of, I used.

Finally I started to replace fear with faith. It begins with your mouth. I knew all of this, but it took some time. I knew about fear and how crippling it can be. I got a message late one night that my mother had gone home to be with the Lord. Fear was standing there staring me in the face, and instantly I embraced and invited it in, only to be tied up by it. I stayed locked up for one year. Yes, for one year I was a slave to fear. It had become very difficult to ever be alone at any time. Every room I went in it had to be well lit.

My husband and I were getting along very well at the time, and I must say he was understanding and patient with me through this. He took me wherever he went so I would never be left alone. Once he had taken on a project out of town for three months, so I moved in with my daughter because I was afraid to stay at home alone. I could not go back in the house by myself to get a change of clothes or anything without someone being with me. I hated my house.

At night it became worse. I would be attacked in my sleep. Most nights I stayed up in fear of having a bad nightmare. Once in my sleep I felt someone trying to choke me, and I could barely get the words out, but I said three times, "Jesus!" Then suddenly it stopped. I didn't realize at the time what had happened. The devil was afraid of me and the anointing on my life. And on top of that, I was learning some powerful things about who I was in Christ. I started to pray for every older person I met, and many of them became born again.

The devil was afraid of what God was doing through me against his satanic kingdom. I was tearing it down, and I was not playing. I was not about to stop. Therefore, he placed something in my path to try and stop me. Back then, I was afraid of death and people that had previously passed away. When I was young I watched horror movies such as *The Night of the Living Dead*. I would dream about it and awaken in fear. I refused to go to funerals because I would be afraid afterward for months. Therefore I tried going to funerals, but avoided viewing the body. That worked okay, but I still just preferred not to go. I liked remembering the departed the way they were.

Since most of the people I prayed for or was close to were the elderly, they would pass on. Therefore, every few months I was cutting an obituary out of the newspaper. After one year of being terrified by the devil with the spirit of fear, God gave me something. The powerful weapon was Psalm 91 — the entire chapter. I started reading it and imprinting it on my heart. I memorized the entire chapter and wrote it down. I took that paper with me wherever I went and held on for dear life. I had a copy in each room of my house; I slept with it under my pillow. I told my children about it and gave them a copy. This weapon was so powerful, it worked while I was asleep!

Here is an unforgettable story that will remain with me always. One evening while I was left at home alone for only a few hours, it grew dark and I began to panic. My husband was great and would call if he knew he would be getting home later than expected, so this was one of the times I got a phone call. He said he was going to be gone for an additional hour. The one hour turned into two, and by now it was pitch black outside. I could not rest and was beside myself walking the floor, back and forth to the door. Darkness came all over me I started to shake and tremble. Then I picked up the Bible starting reading Psalm 91.

That did it. All the sudden, fear started to leave and I began to calm down. As I continued to read that scripture over and over again, confidence rose in me and filled the entire atmosphere. My spirit was finally at peace and the fear was gone forever. Before I knew it, my husband was home and I was thrilled to find out that I had graduated.

Victory was with me all along, if only I would had just picked up the Bible and read Psalm 91. God came through, and now that same God can do the same for you… if you are willing.

Are you ready to graduate?

Every time I heard someone read Psalm 91, I would say, "That is my victory." I can feel every part of me shouting for joy. Fear can be powerful, but the word of God is more powerful. The power of God's word broke the chains of fear that night. The word of God goes to bat for you, so be sure and use this weapon. God does not want His children to live in fear. So many times in the Bible it reads, "Fear not." This is God's desire for the virtuous woman — the woman who is not afraid of bad weather, not afraid to get out there and give to her family, and not afraid to give to the poor. The virtuous woman is not afraid to get up early in the morning, nor is she afraid of anything.

Fear will make you do stupid things. For instance, fear may

drive you to marry someone you just met over the Internet. Fear can cause you to be pressured by your biological clock, with every tick making you feel even more alone and empty. Fear can cause you to stay with a man who tells you he doesn't want you anymore.

That was one of my mistakes. I don't know why I thought I could mold my man into an image I wanted. You cannot change a grown man. He ought to know what he wants, and if he doesn't want you, do not even try to change him. You are better off being by yourself until you can overcome this. Sometimes as women of God we need to take a hard look at ourselves. Be honest; do not try to trick that man into wanting you. You are not all that.

By deceiving him (being something you are not) you become caught in a mess. More people are involved, namely your children, and they become main targets. The job of "fear" is to rob you, intimidate, and distract you from all that God has for you. Its mission is to get you in a position of compromise and confusion so you won't know what to do. You cannot make important decisions when you walk in fear. For instance, you may choose any lawyer, but it may be the wrong lawyer.

Instead, just wait and be still. The rushing will stop. It is not the end of the world, despite the fact that you lost the house, furniture and receive no child or spousal support. God will take care of you and the children. It may be time for you to start over and get all new stuff, so let go all of your old belongings (if you can). It is not worth paying another lawyer a lot of money to fight over something you didn't need in the first place. Although it is part yours, don't be afraid to let it all go. Give it up and follow God if He asks you to. You can replace "things," and these "things" are not going to make you happy.

Your children can live without the reminder of strife in their lives. They just want you safe and happy. Most importantly, they want to see you getting over this. I know it is hard to move on, but once you forget about the life you had with him, you can get over the trauma (and drama). You are going to make it.

It does not matter how bad you look or feel right now. God is going to get you through this. He wants to pick you up, dust you off and start all over again. In God's hands, you will not fail. He is able to keep you. He has a place in His heart for hurting women such as you and me — the woman who has been lied to all of her life and told she is nobody; the woman who has been beaten and talked about. He knows your heart because He has been there. They did the same thing to His son. So God knows and is laughing at those who plot against you.

Do not take the battle in your own hands. Give it to God. He will take care of it. Besides that, it's His job anyway. Do not be afraid to tell God how you really feel, especially if you have been hurt and He knows it. He knows everything, but tell Him anyway. You are his and He cares about what you care about. He is part of you and you are part of Him. That ex-husband is no longer a part of you. God is your number one man.

Do not get a panic attack and decide to go out and find another man to fill the void. Be still and wait on God. Indulge yourself in the things of God, especially now that you have free time. Do not dwell on your old life anymore, for you are moving on and out of the mess.

Get ready to launch out into the deep. God is there waiting on you with a new and better house — one that is paid for. Do not fret, do not worry, and do not be afraid. God is for you He is on your side. Fear is the devil's faith. Do not get caught in that trap. When it comes knocking at your door, do not answer. Ask God to answer the knock, because you work for God and you have his favor.

Do not let fear rule in any part of your life. Believe that God wants to take you out of this, deliver you and set you up.

Receive that freedom now.

BE STILL

BE still and know that God is God. He will never change, but will always remain the same. Be sharp so you will know when things are trying to come against you. God speaks to me in a silent atmosphere. If you are always doing something to keep busy, God may use your sleep hours to speak to you. That is when the mind is pushed aside.

I felt totally lost and did not know what to do. I was not depressed, but I was not happy either. The label I selected was, "I must be going through menopause." That explained it, because I was getting older and the symptoms fit. So I would go with that.

Please do not put on labels God did not give you. You cannot walk this journey the world's way. I did not even know the meaning of menopause, but it made me feel better to find a label (an explanation or excuse). No matter what it looks like around you, continue to stand firm and be still before the Lord. I know at times I got nervous because it seemed I needed to be doing something. I cannot stand being in one place for very long. God dealt with me and I am continuing to learn how to be still.

During the day your life goes on. So as women, I know that it can be difficult because we find so many things to do. Too many of times I had to make myself settle down in my spirit, because I was always pumped up and doing a lot of nothing. I wore myself out and by nighttime was exhausted. I stressed myself out trying to do everything.

I remember going to the doctor because my blood pressure was out of control to the point I needed medication. I didn't realize it at the time, but found it out later. I was having anxiety attacks which caused my blood pressure to rise. At times I was awakening in the night to a pounding in my chest, and after I took a blood pressure pill it slowly stopped. All God wanted from me was to be still. What God was saying to me was, "Slow down and be still." The result is, you are going to make it.

I needed to settle down because God wanted to speak to me. Try not to be so busy about the world's way, instead of being busy in God's way. Remember, His yoke is light. For two weeks I had time to read more, pray more and meditate on God's word. I used that situation to get closer to God. I learned how to pray in tongues for an hour every day. Take short term goals and start out slow. As long as you do it unto the Lord, He will receive it.

Being still before the Lord can sometimes be a struggle. Once you have overcome the hindrances, you can move on, make your way and prosper in the things of God. Things will continue to be frustrating around you, but you won't be in it anymore. God will hide you in a secret place; there you will find the peace of God that surpasses all understanding. In this place you will find everything you need. God will make sure of it. When you become frustrated and worried about things not happening, it steals away what God intends for you. God has given you rest and peace, and has clearly made these tools available.

After my divorce, God put me in a special place of protection. There God said to me, "This is a place of peace and rest; I want you to write a book, a book for women who are on the edge and gone beyond being depressed... women who feel the only way out is to take their life." As I began to write this book, I had a hard time finding peace. Being still was out of the question. Everything I attempted to do outside writing the book was self-destructing. There was an attack from hell against me.

Therefore, with this assignment how was I supposed to find the peace I needed? Each month it got worse. Then I realized that if God put me here and I was having all these things come against me, then something was wrong. Did God make a mistake, or what? The kind of people I was in contact with was mostly Christians, so I was puzzled. Opinions from other Christians were not helpful — they were just what I would call "okay" and nothing more. I wondered if anyone would go out of their way to help me, and I didn't know if I was expecting too much, or what.

I thought I was around people who recognized God's own. However, they didn't — and that surprised me. I thought, "What is wrong with these people in this area? Do they serve the same God I serve, or just don't know any better? Do they have the Holy

Spirit in their lives, and is He being active?" My God! How was I supposed to write a book while worrying about all this going on? I thought seriously about my life then. I thought about the promise God made to the people in Moses' day. God gave his children the Promised Land, which was occupied by someone else at the time. God gave me that same promise when I moved to the area I lived in. Now it is up to me to take it by force.

How we do that is on our knees. We enter into warfare prayer every day. At times, it got so bad I could not write, for too much was going on. I had no job, no income, and yet I knew that this book had to be completed. I had to do more than praying. I knew if I was going to make it, at least I was going to get a book out of it. Women, you have to know that God will get you to that place of promise and keep you safe there. That place happened to be a book in my life.

Be still and know that God is God.

GOD IS FAITHFUL

GOD will never let you down. I feel no worry when I believe Him. Faith is stronger than fear. We all must get to this point when we know without a doubt that God is faithful. He won't lie because he cannot lie. He is the God of truth. If He said it, it will happen.

It may get a little dim and you may think nothing is happening. Your part is to wait, and while you are waiting, start to serve. You just want be able to figure out how God does it. I have been paying my tithe for years. I gave dangerously large amounts of offerings over and above. I was not ashamed to give, because God had taught me early on to be obedient. So it did not seem unusual that I should to obey God in large amounts. I knew my part was to be obedient and give when God told me to. I had no problem with that. I love giving unto God's kingdom. I could not wait until Sunday or Bible Study. As soon as I received a large amount that I could give, I personally made sure it was in my man or woman of

God's hand — which was my Pastor's hand. I wanted to plant it in the ground as soon as possible. After all, I had a marriage that needed to be saved.

Now wouldn't you know, my marriage ended anyway? I heard the devil telling me, "You gave away all the money for nothing." That is what my ex-husband would tell me.

However, the God that I serve is faithful and mighty with all the power in His hands. My simple response was, "I gave unto the Lord, not man." This is what God expected of me. I knew for sure that my prayers and offerings would not go in vain. My prayers are still in effect right now. First I prayed for salvation for my ex-husband and that my marriage would be restored. I believe God answered both, and as for the marriage, it as well — maybe not by the world's standards, but the spiritual marriage with Jesus. God is faithful, and when prayers and offerings go up, the blessings come down. His word will not return to Him void, but shall accomplish what He sent it out to do.

The word of God is sharper than a sword. When you start to say it repeatedly, something happens. Don't give up on God. It is the marriage that failed, and not God. There's no need to blame God.

It is hard for most of us to believe God is faithful when we are going through stuff. No money in the bank? God is faithful. Kids need clothes? God is faithful. Rent is due? God is faithful. Can we really say we believe this? If we don't, then we should, because it is true even when we going through it. He is still faithful and working on our behalf. Start to believe God is faithful before the breakthrough. We should not be surprised when He comes through. He is only doing what He said He would do.

I have no one else to trust but God. I am not married anymore, the devil is a liar, and God is truth. I want God. I had to look ahead and not behind. My new life was waiting for me. A future was calling me. There are many who need to hear my voice. I owed nothing to the devil and my marriage was over. So the devil owes me with great interest, and I am using it to tear down his evil kingdom. My mission is to restore and heal the heart of hurting women, especially those who feel they are hopeless. If this is you, know that God is faithful. He has not forgotten about you. He sent me to tell you to hold on. You are going to make it.

Your cry has not gone in vain. You have been beat down, and God saw it all. He loves you so much. Please, whatever you do, hold on to these words: GOD LOVES YOU.

You are somebody.

There was a high price paid for you

God did not make junk.

Even though it felt like I was not going to make it at times, a few things I remembered that kept me going were:

GOD LOVES ME

GOD DOES NOT LIE

GOD IS FOR ME

With this on your side, breakthrough will come. The worst thing you can do is doubt God. That has to offend Him, just like we are offended when our children do not believe in us. Try to hold on to this. If He has done it once, He can do it again. When trouble comes your way, just say, "God is faithful." Chose to be around people who you know have had God work in their lives, and then say, "If He did it for them, He will do it for me."

Remember, God is the same God yesterday, today and forever.

TIME TO RECEIVE

GET ready to receive! Your harvest is in. Receiving is a gift from God, and not everybody knows or realizes how important it is to being in a position to receive. I like to give, but sometimes I have a problem receiving, especially if I know the giver is going through hard times. I don't want them to take away from themselves, for that makes me feel even worse.

I know now that this is wrong thinking. I learned it is in the giving that you receive. When God anoints you, it is not for you. It is for someone else. When you are married, the wife has an anointing for her husband, and the husband has an anointing for his wife. Problem is, if you don't know that how you can activate something, you won't know how to receive it.

Know that you are worth being a daughter of the King. God wants the best for you. There is a mansion waiting for you. I met a woman who had invested a lot of time helping the elderly when she was younger. Now she had gotten older herself. I reminded her about all the good work she used to do, and she was amazed at how much of an impact she had made all those years ago. She lives in one of the best retirement facilities in her area, with everything paid for. I reminded her that God was rewarding her with a pleasant life style, and that she should receive it.

I remember one Sunday when the tithes and offerings had just been received. The pastor knew a lot of us personally, because our church was small at the time. Therefore, he knew we all had our own financial obligations. However, in addition the pastor asked for another offering, which I thought was selfish at that time. But most all the congregation was in debt and we needed unexpected income, favor and debt release. We needed an anointing to come on us. So we all knew by now that something must be up with God, because our pastor was asking for a second offering when God knew we had a tremendous need ourselves.

We gave and sowed financial seeds. We came out of our comfort zone and gave dangerously over and above. Some of us launched out into the deep and gave what God told us. You cannot expect from God if you have a fear of giving too much. You can never beat God's giving. Out of our obedience, some of us got job promotions, some of our kids starting behaving, and everyone had a testimony.

Now I know why God had the Pastor encourage us to give out

of our need. It was to make our way prosper. If you are in deep financial need, find someone to bless their socks off. The key to receiving is learning how to give; it is in our giving that we receive. Start to expect from God because he is your reward.

Do not expect to receive if you have not been a giver. My mother had always been a giver all her life. When she got older, she got blessed, favored, unexpected income and an anointing of debt release wherever she went, all the time. There was an outpouring of blessing that came over her life. Most times she didn't even need to leave the house, because people she didn't even know or just barely knew would stop by and put money in her hand. That spirit of giving continued on even at her home going and funeral. There were people who traveled from all over just to say good bye. Her legacy still lives on.

I am happy to say my four brothers and five sisters are all givers. It is truly a gift from God to receive the gift of giving. The day of my mother's home going, God taught me about the gift of forgiveness. That is why I can say that today I forgive my ex-husband. It is time to receive and welcome this gift that God has for you.

It is not hard to receive if you have done what the word says: to be kind to others. Put in a request for this gift. Tell God you are ready to make a withdrawal. Just as you give with a cheerful heart, learn how to receive with one. Do not let the devil make you feel guilty and taint your blessings. If we do not receive from God, we can miss more than we think.

One night I had a dream about my salvation, which in turned gave me instructions for my entire life. That dream shaped my future and placed me where I am today. There is a part (one) which is giving and a part (two) which is receiving, but you know how we do tend to leave one or both parts out of it and choose the part we want. When you receive something, it means a light comes on. I received very specific (and difficult) instructions from God concerning my business. I had sought the Lord about which direction I should go. I had let the business get out of control by not making decisions. I turned away for a minute and gave others control. Once I saw what was happening, I stepped back into the picture and got ready to change things, but by then it was too late. The damage was already done. I had no other choice but to address the problem and let them go.

Those were the hardest instructions I received. The person I had to fire was my husband, my mate, and my friend. He had changed and turned into a non-caring, ruthless man, and one that I was not proud of.

Giving and receiving: when we put the two together, they become powerful forces for good. Remember, where there is much given there is much required. This was what was required for me to do. I would rather obey God than to sacrifice the gift of receiving.

Do not let it be a surprise when God asks you to do something you don't understand, or gives you're something beyond your comprehension. It is your time to receive because you have been faithful. You stood the test and didn't give up when asked to do a task in obedience to GOD. Therefore, God will reward you when it is your season. No matter how long you think it may be, He always shows up on time. Right when you are at the door, don't give up. Continue on. You have made it this far, so be ready for yours. It belongs to you.

I don't know how God does it, but He does. I had no problem receiving, because I knew it was my time. We all have set times. For me, if my time would have come sooner I would have not realized and understood the gift of receiving and how to cherish it. Now I cherish this gift of receiving because I know what I had to go through to get it. You can receive a gift that you know God wants you to have. He gives us gifts all the time because he loves us.

There is another gift that God wants us to receive. Remember, receiving means you own it. It is yours and it belongs to you. It is a gift that God wants you to have — the gift of salvation. This gift keeps on giving it is an everlasting gift, a gift you can enjoy and rejoice over.

CHAPTER SEVEN

REJOICE AND ENJOY

REJOICE! For this is the day that the Lord has made. I will rejoice and be glad in it. Psalm 118:24 tells us this is a time to rejoice, for God has made us glad. You still have a lot of work to do, so get ready for the blessings of God to flow continually. Take a minute and put your legs up, this is your time. The sacrifices have been many. God is able. He did it, and so I know to whom the Glory and honor goes. Enjoy the rest of your life and don't let burdens weigh you down anymore.

You deserve to be happy now, if you are at this point after your divorce. Most people never make it to a place of victory after all the tricks and games that go on. God will interrupt your pity party and bless you above anything you can imagine. Then He will give you something to be glad about. He is getting you ready to go to that place so you can enjoy the good life.

You probably thought this day would never come, but it is here. The people you started out with may not end up with you, but God has a way of bringing everyone back into your life, especially the ones who need to be there. You have trusted him this far, so don't give up now. Sometime it is hard for others to understand why you are happy. Some people you have not spoken to in years may call you unexpectedly.

Be ready for anything and don't be caught off guard. Let no one steal your joy. Start out singing in the morning and go to bed singing at night. Let it be a time of victory — claim it and take it by force. This time is set aside just for you. Rejoicing makes the devil mad and he cannot figure out why his tricks are not working. The memory of having a picnic comes to mind: people coming to eat good food and enjoy themselves and just have fun. People will be drawn because they want to know what the fuss is all about. It will also give you the opportunity to give your testimony. Let everyone know what the Lord has done for you. They won't look at you the same, but they will know you have something that they don't have.

One Sunday I walked into Sunday school with a glow on my face, just happy to be alive. The teacher asked me what had happened. "Did you get a job? Are you working yet?" he asked. I said no. He looked puzzled and could not figure out what I was so happy about. He also happened to be my counselor, so he was aware of what I was going through. He had prayed with me before about my finances.

Anyway I didn't look like I should be rejoicing about anything. However, he was stunned by the expression on my face. He had assumed that I had gotten the greatest job with the best pay, but all I had was the joy of the Lord — and no job or anything else can do that. It was Jesus.

My daughter asked how I could write a chapter on rejoicing after everything that was happening to us. We had both lost our vehicles and had no transportation, with barely enough money to pay our bills. "So how are you going to write about rejoicing?" she asked. I had to, because this has been part of my healing. Yes, I must agree it was a challenge. As a matter of fact, it took one month to finish. Each day I would sit down to write, and there was NOTHING.

Day after day went by. Still nothing. I would fall asleep with my notebook in my hand and wake up to blank pages. I would rather do anything then to go back to those empty pages. I got a new CD and listened to praise and worship to stimulate my mind. I had a deadline, and it was getting close. I knew if God wanted this assignment finished, He would give me what I needed. I was inviting so many distractions in, it soon started to smother what God wanted me to do.

You do not have to think long and hard. Your reasons to rejoice are right there in front of you. Believe in your heart that

God has already done everything for you. That alone is enough to be glad about.

Are you glad that Jesus loves you?

Have a picnic, invite someone over, and tell him or her that Jesus loves them. Let it be said by your neighbors, "All I know is one thing about her — she is always happy and has a smile on her face." Let your attitude flow all over the neighborhood. I knew people who could only rejoice when they had money or things were going well. Can money have the power to change your mood?

If you are happy, then you are happy. That is all there is to it, and it does not change. I realize we sometimes may tend to forget that, because we are not perfect. It seems we are controlled by the circumstance and not by God. It takes us over and we end up getting depressed over money. Well, the money may come and go. I want to be happy, regardless. If you hold onto that idea long enough, God will fulfill your desires.

Start to rejoice at the beginning and thank Him beforehand. Let your faith work. Exercise it and see it grow. Go out on a limb as I did, and believe all things are possible through Jesus Christ. He will never let me down no matter what it looks like, nor will He let you down. Do not let doubt and unbelief rob you of what God has done for you. He did it once, and He can do it again.

Take this opportunity and be glad. Try to find something to rejoice about. Just say, "I want to banish gloom and doom through this process." Take it when you get it. The opportunity is yours. Do not be afraid to step into it and enjoy.

LIVING HOLY

LIVING a holy lifestyle should always be a part of your spiritual existence. How you conduct yourself — and not just around church folks — matters. Do you always need to tell people how bad your marriage was? People should not have to ask if you are a Christian or not. From the first sentence out of your mouth, they will know.

Your words should line up with your life. What you plant in your heart (the ground) will come up. Living holy means doing what is right and true, even when you are being done wrong. You can see through a phony person. The reason most unbelievers do not want to be a Christian is because they are watching Christians who are not living holy. Make sure you are not a poor example, because then nobody will want to be like you.

Are you complaining all the time whenever someone sees you? Are you forcing captive audiences to listen to your sad story? Be sensitive and remember that there is a time and place for everything. If your lifestyle is not "all that," people will notice. They are looking for clues that make you, as a Christian, different from them. Do you exemplify Christ if:

I go to the club — you go to the club.

I go with a married man —you go with a married man.

I curse every now and then — you curse every now and then.

If so, you do not have anything they want. On the other hand, show them a holy lifestyle and they will see that God has something better for their futures. Through you, they will see the power and joy that comes with serving God in holiness. They will witness you in action:

Someone steals from you — walk in forgiveness.

Someone does not have any money — treat him or her to a meal.

Someone is going through a similar situation — take time to listen to them.

Someone is doing something wrong — you know better and refuse to do it.

What example are you living? Are you causing your brothers and sisters to fall? Are you encouraging un-Godly behavior? If so, God will let you know that He is not pleased. Once God checked me on my relationship with my sister. If you have heard the phrase "too spiritual and no earthly good," well, that was me when it came to my sister. She was not saved at the time and was living with her boyfriend. I had just been born again and thought I could preach to her. God set me down and let me know that I could not change her. It was not my job. My job was to accept her as my sister and love her. I started sharing with her by simply loving her and not judging. I could see the change that came over our relationship. I think she was beginning not to like me very much, and so this turned our relationship around.

In my private time I started praying for her, and then two months later my sister told me she had gotten saved and was going to church. A few more months passed and the boyfriend left. Therefore, you see, God did not need any help on my part. It was simple. I was to love my sister and not judge her, but pray for her. God had a time set just for her to bring her close to himself.

What I am saying is we are not perfect. We make mistakes. We do the same thing in our marriages. If your husband is messed up, what makes you think you are all right? There is no such thing as a perfect marriage. There is something wrong with all of us. No matter who we are, we all have issues. Jesus didn't come to save the perfect, for no one is perfect. He came to save me and you.

Just like working on a marriage, you have to work every day at living right in the eyes of the Lord. You cannot do it one day and then just stop trying. God has a 24-hour watch on us. And so does the enemy, who is also observing us.

We Christians are Christ Ambassadors, so your example may be the only one most people ever see. Remember, we are not perfect, but we are called to do better than most. We have a higher standard. Let Godly living become a part of your everyday lifestyle. If you hope to marry again, this is what will draw him. The way you treat others and the way you live, and most of all, the way you love God will "tell on you" every time. It is like crystal that will shine right through you.

If you are hiding the real you, this is when it will show up. Let your lifestyle become a testimony to the world. By looking your best and acting your best with the love of God rooted and grounded in you, you are sharing this part of your life in the best possible light. And that extends to all aspects of our lives. Make sure your car looks good and your house looks good. Many people just keep the main rooms of their house clean, while their bedrooms are a mess. Stay holy not just when people are watching, but even when no one is watching but you and God.

When you are at home hollering at your kids, check yourself and live holy.

At the grocery store, live holy.

At the post office, live holy.

In Walmart, live holy.

When you have to face your ex-husband, live holy.

Do not let it just be lip service. Let people see what you are made of everywhere you go. And be careful, because some things just do not line up with holiness, like buying lottery tickets and listening to foul-mouthed comedians. What music do you listen to? Does is glorify violence and dirty talk about sex, drugs and alcohol? How do you even expect to live in the abundance if you are engaging in such things? The abundance is watching and waiting to reward you as you live holy. Don't let earthly temptations or "peer pressure" snatch it away.

WALKING IN THE ABUNDANCE

THE overflow is about to happen when all hell breaks loose. Day after day, some new person gets ready to rob you. That I know for sure. People will try to take money from us over the silliest things. Before I lost my car, I remember taking it in for a basic checkup. It was not even a year old, and the mechanic told me I need all new tires. How typical, and I had some different rip-off attempt happen every day. For instance, my insurance over charged me and would not refund my money, even after realizing they had made an error. Then the doctor overcharged me on an account that should have only been half the amount.

This is only to name a few, but this was how I knew that I was walking in the overflow. The devil might know about your blessings before you do! He is not sure what will work, so he tries it all. Whatever you are left with, he wants that, as well. This is your indicator that now you are living in the abundance of God. You are the righteousness of God. Be ready for the attacks and keep your armor on. The enemy is not just going to stand by and do nothing. We are continually in warfare, even more so since you have gotten this far.

As I wrote my last two chapters, I was in and out of bed trying to retain my energy to do what I had to do. My blood pressure went up and down and I became weak at times. Days would pass when I could not do anything but stay in bed and rest. My daughter brought my meals to me and took care of me. She kept me encouraged and reminded me of the vision to get this book out to the women who needed to hear my voice.

All of this will come if you stay in the race; do not give up, because you will make it. Learn how to stay focused on what God is doing, and not the enemy. God is going to take care of your every need, even when it looks like it is not going to happen. Start to press in and take what you know belongs to you.

The abundant life belongs to you. Do not allow the enemy to steal this, too.

I knew something was about to happen because of the attacks I was getting. The abundance is more than enough. It is meant to bless you over and above. You will not be limited to just paying your bills off. There are souls out there who need to hear the Gospel. Finances have to come through the hand of someone who is not afraid to think higher than "just enough." Start to see yourself in a large mansion and thousands of people won to the Lord because of your obedience to give unto God's Kingdom.

I am so ready for that. I do not think I could write this chapter if I could not see myself walking in the abundance. I already know it is coming not only for me, but also for you if you are reading this book. God has put this book in the hands of someone (you) who needs to hear the words, "You are next." God is saying, "It is your turn, child of God."

That is why you can thank God in advance of a blessing. You have waited and been patient without complaining. I have listened to pastor's talk about just having enough and lives that have become generic. Finish high school, get a degree or learn a trade, buy one house and two cars — the typical life. This seems only one step away from poverty. I want to be like Peter. My net is so full of fish that I will call my neighbors and call all the boats around me to come and get some of what I have. Be willing to share your wealth with others. When God called you, it was to bless all those around you.

Along with this abundant life, also ask God for wisdom. Part of my process was to realize that God had something greater for me. I had let myself get so beat down that I had problems with the abundance. "Is this real?" I asked myself. "You mean, I am making progress? You mean, I am still in my right mind? You mean, God still loves me?" The answer to these questions is — yes.

YES!

Because you are not afraid to think higher than the ordinary, you have leapt into a completely new lifestyle. I never wanted to bring attention to myself. I just wanted to live a low profile kind of life with some financial freedom. As I looked at all the famous movie stars and actors while standing in line at the grocery store, I noticed one of the gossip magazines at the checkout counter. The headline mentioned something about a person who had just gotten a show — something written to hurt this person by targeting feelings and emotions. It read, "**Blank** is a fraud." I thought, "How sad that is. I would hate people to say those terrible things about me."

I knew when I wrote this book that I had opened my heart to minister to hurting women, and not everyone was going to like what I had to say. Someone could write a nasty headline and do the same thing to me. I knew the risk and I thought about all the stories. I have heard about publishers that take all your money and the book then leave you with nothing.

But I had to write this book no matter what, that I knew for sure. However, the other part, I had to admit, I was not so sure of. I had to think about that for a few days. God knew my heart; it was for Him to use me to help hurting women who are just about ready to end it all. I am talking about desperately hurting women —it is these wounded souls to who I am called to minister. If this is you, please let me remind you that I am one person who hears you. I care. I know how you feel, which is very much like I felt. You are worth something to God even if you cannot squeeze out a prayer right now. He cares for you. Do not let anyone tell you that you are not special to Him. You can count on His love for you.

After my few days of thinking about what I was getting myself into, there was no doubt in my heart and mind. Actually, there was never a doubt; you see, it is not me anymore. It is Christ within me, and He is the one who put it inside of me from the beginning. I could not stop even if I wanted to. God has sealed it in there. In my heart is a desire to see hurting women get to a point of trusting God to heal them.

Once your healing process has begun, do not go back to your past hurts. God will give you a time to grieve. Do not use this time forever. The overflow is not just money. It is a lot more than that. When you see the many of souls coming to Jesus, you are walking a path that pleases the Lord. Therefore, I will not worry if people do not like me. When they hate you, they hate the Christ in you, so I will not take it personally. God will shield you so none of the arrows get through.

Walking in the abundance, you have to know that God has spoken to you and you must not waver. It will keep you on the path to fulfill the calling. You may be right at the door, and circumstances may happen that tempt you to leave your post. Be on guard and stand firm.

I went to Church one Sunday. The Pastor was ministering on finding your place in the Church and being about God's business. What he touched on briefly was that God is anchoring us, while being our refuge. When God has you hidden, He takes you to a place of rest. I could have easily taken what he said out of context and got involved in a position at Church, which would have moved me away from my post. See, I knew what God had already told me beforehand. Many times I have been tempted to move from this place in life where God has placed me. It has been hard at times, staying in this place. What got me through is knowing what God told me. What God is telling you may be different.

I recommend you get a diary and a ledger. You need a diary to write down your personal feelings and a ledger to write down your dreams. Keep a good record of everything you are going through. You never know, it could help someone else. You still have so much to give, and now you have the experience of going through a divorce. This means you have gained wisdom while making it through a difficult time, and now you are living in the abundance.

GIVE THANKS

PLEASE do not forget to give thanks. Tell God "thank you" for keeping you. You have a lot to be thankful for. Something good has come out of all this, and you have won the victory. Put your praise on and have a HALLELUJAH party. This will paralyze the enemy, because he thought he had canceled you out. Now you have gotten past all the traps and are in a position to be telling God "thank you."

Say out loud, "It is too late now, devil! You have lost." Let him know he is a loser. You serve a good God — one who deserves the praise. Start to thank God even if you don't see the manifestation. Just act like you have it already. This is a precious time for you, so use it well. Start by spending time in union with the Lord. Do not miss this time of remembering how good God has been, and by all means, continue to be thankful! I can hardly count the numerous times God has kept me from harm. Where would I be if it were not for Him?

Someone once told me once that prayer means 3/4 giving thanks and the rest is for asking. Notice there is a lot more time spent in thanking God. For some reason God is more interested in how we react to Him blessing us. Sometime we are ungrateful and don't give God the time we should in thanking Him. We have not had a grateful heart when it comes to God's turn, because we want it to be about us. It's me, me, me, all the time. We put ourselves first, then God second. This means the idol we have made is of ourselves.

My mother trained her children to be polite. I remember being embarrassed if I didn't do this. The older women in my neighborhood would also make sure all of us children were on our best behavior. This was a big deal to them, but meant very little to us. I think we still sometimes do not think it is a big deal when God blesses us. I think most people may feel that God owes it to them, so there is no need.

If we are treating God this way, we need to stop and thank Him. Momma use to say, "It does not cost anything to speak and say thank you." How much does it cost for us to be grateful and spend a few minutes giving thanks every day? This is especially true when getting up in the morning and before going to bed at night — give thanks. I would think of my children if they were not with me and wonder where they were and what they were doing. My son, being in the military, traveled, so many times his days were my nights. When my children were small, I tucked them in their beds and we would all say good night to each other two or three times until finally everyone had gotten their share. Here is what we started out saying:

Good night (me) — say your prayers.

My children — Okay, Mom, good night! I love you.

(Me) — I love you too.

It was just like the Walton's on television, and throughout their lives I was always thankful knowing my children were safe.

Across the street right in front of my house was a tall streetlight with a bright glow shining into our window. That light provided a night light in case we need to get up during the night. I am truly thankful that I have that same light shining in my life today. Back then, I referred to it as my protection, but I know now that it was the light of the Lord shining bright on my children and me. I am thankful for the light back then and the light that I have now.

It really helped me to think about the goodness of the Lord and how He kept watch over us. The process that I have gone through will never be forgotten. Is some place in your life empty? Learn to fellowship with God by giving thanks. He is the only one who is worthy, and the only one who should be lifted up and exalted above all things. God knows what it is going to take for you to get where you need to go. Leave that man alone and let God handle him. Instead, trust God by letting Him be Lord. He loves you. Do not forget to give thanks.

CHAPTER EIGHT

COMPLETING THE PROCESS

THE number 7 is a sign of completion, and the number 8 is a new beginning. You are at number 8 now. The hardest part is over. I knew you could do it! Now you know without a shadow of a doubt that you are going to make it. All of your emotions have been used. You used some you didn't even know you had. You learned how to cry how to be happy and how to live. You have completed the process.

The opportunity to heal from your divorce is ready now. What you see now is a product of a strong woman who has been developed into the likeness of Christ. Something has happen and it's all good. You are a new creature who has a new walk and talk. You are no longer locked up inside. Instead, you are free. Yes, you are free, so now rejoice!

This is only part of the task that has reached completion. The book has been finished, and now the real work begins. It is going to always be task in front of us, but different for each one of us.

I have met many older people who are bored and have gotten depressed over the years because they consider themselves eliminated from the task of being needed. Since growing older, their lives sometimes seemed unappreciated and worthless. Their children now do everything for them, and they are living in a nursing home ready and wanting to die. Some don't even have families anymore, or maybe just a distant relative or friend.

I recently visited an elderly man in the nursing home. He had no family or friends and was diagnosed with diabetes. One leg was recently amputated. The doctors had expected him to die. My daughter-in-law worked in the nursing home and noticed that this gentleman never had any visitors come to see him. So she told me about him and I was lead to visit him from time to time. He started to show improvement after each visit. It doesn't take much to show people you care; it may not mean anything to you, but it sure means a lot to them. This man's life still had worth. He looked so much like my Dad, and we became friends. The nursing home reported to me that I was his only visitor, except for his caseworker. I took my entire family to meet him; they were all amazed at how much he looks like our Dad.

You are a benefit to someone all the time. You can find something to do and somewhere to start. Sometimes we can be right on target until we're all used up and have nothing left for the people in need. Start with the ones who are close to you in your home and neighborhood. Sometimes this can be the most difficult, but it is the most needed. I remember feeling guilty when every Saturday I volunteered to do prison ministry for youth, but yet I had the same teenagers in my neighborhood and in my home who needed the same encouragement.

There will be times when you just don't know what to do. I first tried to make myself available to my teenage grandchildren, and then I wanted to reach their friends as well, but not scare them away. None of them showed any interest... or so I thought. But what I failed to realize was they were watching and checking me out to see what was working for me. Here I was, thinking I was supposed to see results right away. But sometimes it doesn't work like that.

The girls in the prison were locked up and were very receiving. They would catch on immediately. It was a lot different at home. It was more of a struggle, and when the friends came around they just stayed in the background. Really, all it took for me was to just remember to be kind, loving and understanding. I knew they would eventually come around, so in the meantime we can still minister by the way we act and the way we treat others... and, of course, your lifestyle.

Remember, don't forget to use everything that God gives you for the ministry. If you can remember one thing, remember this:

you are working for God. So pick up the paper that flew in someone else's yard, and not just your yard. Sometimes mow their grass when you are doing yours. Many people think that the only ministry is in the pulpit. But there is always something to do in ministry. Ministry goes on 7 days a week, 24 hours a day. Your job, your home, the grocery store, doing sports — everything you do ministers to someone.

That is why most people label Christians as being phony, because they act one way at church and another way at home. They may have even seen you praising and worshiping God on Sunday, and cursing them out on Monday. Do not get stale. Stay spiritually fresh. If you have gone this long without watching dirty movies, don't start now. If your neighbor tells you off, do not be led to fight. Just because you have finally gotten your first date doesn't mean you should have sex with him.

Finish the process by living as you should and being the Godly example you ought to be. This was my "grieving process," I called it. You decide how it affects you by your lifestyle. The process will come to completion on its own, if you follow a protocol. The protocol is determined by God. He has already predestined you before the foundation of the earth was made. It's up to us to discover it.

Most of us tend to overlook God and come up with our own plans. But we must take the time to complete the process, which includes God's plans. In my opinion, it's not part of the process to be involved in a relationship right now. Allow God to do a work in you before you invite someone in. This is not the time to do nothing or to party, but to stay focused. There will be times for that so don't lose heart.

I strongly recommend to anyone: please wait and complete the grieving process. However long it will take depends on you. You can start by going at least one year after your divorce without getting involved. You owe this to yourself. This is healthy medicine for you, and I want your next time to be the last time. I like to encourage others and let you know now that you can do it.

What about sex?

What about talking?

About one month after my separation, I had a strong desire to be intimate with my husband. I was dreaming about him and thinking, "Now what am I going to do?" I prayed and asked God to help me. As for the dreams, I anointed myself with oil before bed, prayed, repented and kept my Bible under my pillow. I also cried a lot. Three months into the separation, we had an anniversary. I thought about him and thought about him... oh, what I would have given to just to hear his voice.

Three days after our anniversary, God allowed it. He had gotten a hold of my new phone number and called me. God had already revealed to me the things that would dominate the conversation:

He would ask what I was doing.

He would want something from me.

He would indicate that he was full of anger.

His demeanor would prove that he had not changed.

My husband wondered how I was making it; since he made sure he took all our money from me. Do not be tricked into something you are not ready for. After the process, there is a reward. You get peace, joy and happiness. The book may be over, but my life had just begun.

KEEPING A BALANCE

SO much has happened and is happening in your life, and you need to keep a balance. It is so easy to get off course. Remember, you have the tools inside of you. You need to work at it every day and remind yourself that God loves you. Do not take matters in your own hands. That is why we have a God who is good and wants to take care of us. Remember, our parents would tell us after we had done something they didn't like, "Now remember, you are not too old for me to put you over my knee." It's the same with God. We will still get checked by Him, which helps us with our walk. He does it because He loves us.

I try and always maintain a balance. I do not want to be so spiritual that I cannot talk to people without feeling their pain. I know what God promised — He will never leave me, nor forsake me. Occasionally I get those moments when I would like my phone to ring or think about going out on a date. I do not weigh myself down with those continual thoughts. I put them on a scale and ask myself if it lines up with God's word. Is it pure? True? Right or praise worthy? I choose to trust God. He is the best friend I will ever have. I am so glad that I have Jesus, because in the end God's word outweighs everything.

The first year after my divorce was the most critical one regarding what I did and how I carried myself. If you take the proper time, you can organize your feelings and emotions according to what God wants you to do. He will carry you if you let him, until you are strong enough to go on.

God will nurture you until you are ready to fly again. Do not expect to make a living out of it. Just like our natural parents have to push us out of the nest, we all need a spiritual nudge. You will know when you are ready. I would not worry about it right now. Only start to think seriously about if it lingers over a year.

I once knew a man whose wife left him, along with their children. The husband had been abusing the wife physically and mentally for years. Finally, she couldn't take it any longer. She left that city and got a divorce. Years had gone by with no contact with him, nor did he contact the children except for the oldest son, now a teenager, who no longer wanted to live by his mother's rules. He ended back living with the Dad. The woman remarried and moved onto a better life. In the meantime, the husband moved another woman in their home. He made a scene of everything his wife left. Year after year, he was still stuck in that old life.

Now you can clearly see what had happened. He never went through his grieving process to the end. Another problem — or mistake — is that he invited another woman in and made her life just as miserable in the process. The other woman finally left, as well. Now the children are older and grown with children of their own. The main conversation is still the same after all the time had passed. He was still saying, "You know my wife left me." They were in their 30s when they parted, and both are now in their 70s. The last I heard of him, his conversation was still the same: "You know my wife left me."

It is better to get over this now and not hold on any longer than you have to. Allow God to help you. He is the only one who can.

Don't keep talking about your past. It may end up your future. Now stay focused on what God wants for you, because it is always good. When you are keeping things in balance, the truth always outweighs the lie. Try it. No matter what it is, weigh it against God's word. The truth will prevail every time, then kick the lie right out. It is up to you. Who do you want to believe? Let your words line up with God's word. Jesus prayed to the Father and referenced the words we should use in John 17:8: "For I have given unto them the words which thou gavest me; and they have received them and have known surely that I came out from thee and they have believed that thou didst send me." Follow Jesus' example that is already laid out before us.

I think everyone knows by now that you have just gone through one of the most terrible divorces imaginable. God wants us to be whole with nothing missing, nothing lacking or broken. We need to stop complaining and act like our example. Learn a new vocabulary. In the middle of something going on, say "Nevertheless, not my will, but God's will be done."

You will need to go a step further than most, so go that extra mile. As you continue to grow, you will find out something new about yourself every day. There were times when it seemed I was going in circles, and then suddenly saw myself changing and moving on. Keep a balance and do not toss to and fro.

SHARING AND CARING

I use to think that everyone on television or those who had written books were extraordinary people. I assumed that not just "anyone" could do what they do. Well, I am a real, regular person just like you. God called me to write this book, and I knew He would do the rest. As for what to do after the writing... well, I had part of the picture, but not completely. So I was obedient and have done what I knew my part to be, and continued being the person I am.

I care about the hurt and pain women go through, and sharing a part of my life may in some way help them realize that they are not alone. I stayed in the boundaries God had chosen for me, and within those limits I knew God had ordered.

I had the opportunity to visit one of my sisters for a few days. She lived three hours away. I knew that God had ordered me to be there for a reason. My sister wanted me to visit all the people she hung out with and old friends we had grown up together with, but I knew my mission at that time. Even though those people needed to hear a kind word of encouragement, it was not time. God will continue to cover you, you but you must be able to sense the spiritual warfare going on. If I had gone out of God's will, I might have actually lost them because of my disobedience. So stay on course with God's plan, no matter the situation. Just walk in love, be slow to speak and quick to listen. That is what I did. Then I went back home and prayed for them.

I think it is good if we don't have the entire picture yet. If we did, we would probably mess things up. It's better to be guided by faith, and not by sight. Just go with what you know and let God handle the rest. Share the love of God by doing things that will help others overcome obstacles they are facing. Just remember, you are the example. Share a part of you that you never shared before. Do not have the same old stories to tell people. Let them know that you care, and be "tangible" about it. If you have gone through a divorce, please listen very carefully as you read this next passage:

You run into someone who tells you they are going through a divorce. You talk with them and find out more than you asked for. As you leave that person, you pat them on the back and say, "Well, if you ever need anything or if there's anything I can do for you, please let me know." Church people and family members may mean well. But by the second time I had this happen to me, I became angry. Those words were customary, but not necessarily sincere.

The truth about the woman going through the divorce? She has been torn inside out. Her finances have been interrupted. She is wounded and hurt. You know at least this much is going on.

So... I dare you to consider the following:

I dare you to hand the woman a check before you say the customary words. Trust me, she needs something, so I also dare you to get her address and phone number. I dare you to pray with her and let God direct you regarding the needs of this person. You already know the basics, because you have gone through it yourself already. The basic needs are:

Love and compassion

Money

Restorations

I beat myself up because I felt no one loved me, and I felt I was a failure. So you can imagine how appreciative I was when someone mailed me a card or wrote me a poem. This blessed me in ways those "customary words" could not. If the Lord leads, people should tuck money in their envelopes. That is truly putting yourself in a wounded person's shoes. Just do it. Do the right thing and be a blessing to a woman who is hurting.

Do not speak negative words about her ex-husband. Just listen. Do not agree with anything she says negatively about her ex-husband. Just be present and let her vent. If you live near her, invite her out to lunch and pay for it. Take her shopping and buy her an outfit. Pay for nails, hair, or a day at the spa. Offer to get her car an oil change. All of these things helped me the most. Please do not sit back and do nothing. Even if you just pray, that is better than nothing.

In the spirit, this is what is happening when you get a divorce. First, you are joined together by God and you now become one. God honors marriage. It is an honorable institution in His sight. In a divorce there is a tearing that separates you, so you are no longer bone of his bone or flesh of his flesh. The spiritual picture I have in my mind is similar to the separation of conjoined twins. But rather than a surgical separation, divorced couples do through spiritual separation. It is a horrendous, painful experience, so please reach out and care as you share.

YOU ARE GOING TO MAKE IT

YOU made it, and I knew you would! During the last month of my marriage, I knew that God was getting me ready for something. I felt bad for my situation, and I feel even worse for the situations of other women who find themselves facing divorce. I could see women just like me and they were all hurting, especially women in ministry. Theirs was a silent hurt.

Not until after I stepped out of my marriage did God show me their hearts. They were hiding behind their husbands; some were even wives of Pastors. I knew God was raising up in me a woman of virtue and character. No matter how bad my husband treated me, I took it with a smile knowing there was a purpose behind the pain.

I feel like a new person since writing this book. I must say it was God — all God. He is the victor in it all. I look back for one last time as I say goodbye, because I made it by realizing the following:

It is OK to cry / as I Let Go And Let God / To Fully Trust God /

by giving Praise and Worship / while During Hard Times / in spite of it Life Still Goes On / even In A Time Of Despair / How Did I Go On / because I was Feeling All Alone / I know God Is My Refuge / I started to Put My Life In Order / The Love Of God / as I Took My Time / I had to Cut Old Ties / as I tried to Protect Myself / I did not want To Faint / because Joy Came In The Morning / then I Found My Place / I Spent Time In Prayer / Promotion came / as I Did The Right Thing / I continued to Walk In Confidence / by Not Being Afraid / Being Still before the Lord / because God Is Faithful / My Time To receive / I started to Rejoice And Enjoy the good life / Walking In the Abundance / I Gave Thanks / Completing The Process / by Keeping A Balance / and through Sharing And Caring I made it.

My goal in this book is to reflect on the woman. Women of God, this is directly from my heart to yours. How God dealt with me and the feeling and emotions I felt was very personal. Every woman is different, and God will attend to your individual needs, but we do have some things in common. The one that stands out is if you dearly love the Lord and have a heart to see women change (and your life change), then we are sisters. This is the journey that I have taken during the first year after my divorce. God started me out with Psalm 37 and I will end with Psalm 37. I pray you make this part of your life every day existence.

Remember, with God's help... YOU ARE GOING TO MAKE IT!

JUST BEING ME

I'VE never been one to pretend nor put on airs, because there was no one I wanted to impress. I figured that life was too short, so why waste it? I discovered recently that friends my age can be a little boring; most of them have settled. They are on tons of medication, and exercise is totally out of the question. Ask them about a self-help book, and they have never heard of it.

I just like being and doing "ME." Following that kind of lifestyle is not for me, although it's okay for whomever it works for.

One summer I decided to take a swimming class at our local pool. I paid for my class and thought it would be fun to ask a family member and friend to join me, as well. I offered to pay, since it was my idea. All I got was, "No, I don't think so because I'm afraid of water." I like trying new things all the time — fun things that don't cost much and don't take long to learn.

The next attempt was to learn how to skate. Again, I asked a different set of people my age and got, "No, I don't think so."

Last but not least, I've always wanted to go on a cruise, so I paid for my portion. The agent thought it would be fun and cheaper if I asked a friend, which would spare me from having to pay for a full room. I thought about it and realized it would be nice to save a little money. I just knew it wouldn't be hard to find a friend to room with me, but I only had two weeks to book someone. After asking several friends my age, all of them said, "No, I'm afraid of water." As the deadline for my final payment approached, my agent asked if I found anyone. He wanted to know how to charge me. I ended paying for a full room without a companion. Now this invitation gets better. I checked around one last time, but now offered a free paid in full cruise to a friend or family member. They were still not interested. I went on the cruise alone enjoyed myself so much can't wait to go back again. I like being me.

God made me very different from anyone else. You can search high and low and will never find another YOU. Your age doesn't define you. It doesn't matter how old you are — it's what you make out of your life. I don't let my age define who I am. At the age of 40, my true identity came alive. For instance, I embraced flowers, gardening and classical music. I never cared about this before, but now all the sudden I just loved it. Every chance I can get, this is what I do. I'm fulfilled just being me, and loving it.

I will never forget my first visit to the music symphony. I was working for a family who had season tickets. They knew how I loved that kind of music, and one weekend an extra ticket became available. Bless them, they wanted me to have it, and it became the opportunity to be introduced to my new found interest in classical music. The legacy had begun. This family was amazed to see a black person so involved in "their music" (as they called it). But that night it became my music, as well. Each day I went to work I put a different CD in and listened during my down time, from one CD to another. I filled that little two bedroom assisted living apartment with classical music every day. Whenever the family would give me gifts. It would be some kind of music or a gardening book.

At home my husband only listened to 70s or R&B music. We were totally different when it came to music. I would lock myself away and listen to gospel contemporary music. Since I was the praise and worship leader at church, I was always looking for anointed music to learn and sing. I guess it worked out okay, because we came together in other areas. He was still my husband and we loved each other the best way we knew how at the time. As I look back, I can appreciate the differences because it taught me a lot.

It's okay to be different. That's probably what drew you together in the first place. Your husband may never tell you, but he may tell others. Once it shocked me to hear him say such nice things about me. I heard him tell some friends, "You will never find anyone who can do their job better than Lucille. When it comes to her elderly patients, she's the best." I could hardly believe it. It pays to be who you are and do what you were born to do. Walk in your destiny discover who you are. Take every opportunity and allow GOD to show you. This will take some time. In fact, it may take years, but that's where patience comes in. You will need to be patient. Don't rush God; His timing is not the same as yours. Just hold on to the fact that God loves you and He wants to heal you of the hurt... if you let Him.

Learning to appreciate the beauty in flowers and gardening has been good for me. My elderly friend was also a member of the local garden club, and something began to stir in me. Flowers became my friends. I knew very few names of flowers and plant, but it wasn't long before I learned something different about each one. We spent time visiting green houses and local nurseries. We watched gardening shows on television and looked at gardening magazines — anything that would give us insight on how to care for her beautiful flower garden. Even though she lived in an assisted living complex, the facility gave us special permission to do our own gardening on the grounds.

Everything I learned, I took home. I spent hours among my flowers getting them just right for planting and replanting. After I filled my front yard, I started on the side. Although living in a rented house took away some of my zeal, I knew one day we would our own home. One evening as I was planting flowers and pulling weeds from the side of my house, it was if God was right there with me speaking to me: "Don't limit yourself. Treat this garden as if it's your very own." It wasn't long before God blessed us with our very own home with big front and back yards, spacious enough to plant all the flowers I wanted. And in the back there was enough room to plant a vegetable garden. I spent hours outside working both. My husband began to notice how happy it made me. Little did I know, this would be the one and only year I had in my house, and it would soon be taken away as my life came tumbling down.

My white picket fence life and my marriage was over. But

even so, I remained the same. I still love flowers, gardening and classical music. Just because things are changing around you, it doesn't mean you have to change being who you are.

Circumstances happen so we can grow. I am talking about the beauty GOD places inside of you and the love you have for His nature. I can't change the fact that I am who I am, and that's all there is to it. I'm very close to all my grandchildren, but one of them inherited some of my personal traits. So whenever the other grandchildren want something extra from me, they have the one who is most "like me" ask. I'm smart enough to know when she comes to me with something that's not for her. I realize the others put her up to it. If you stay the same long enough, you know their character and they know yours. They know "what's you" and "what's not you."

At the time, I wanted to somehow move away from the predictability mold. I feel honored to be the way I am, but just wanted to try something different to see the response. One day I decided to wear black finger nail polish, just because I liked it. Some of my friends frowned at me. The next time I went to Red Lobster with my sisters, I decided to order a mixed drink. One of my sisters told the waitress make sure it's without alcohol. Then I made the comment, "No, make it with the alcohol because without alcohol it just tastes like an Icee." How I shocked my sisters—they were sure I would never choose a drink with alcohol! It's still good being me, even while breaking the mold every so often.

YOU might not realize it, but people are watching you. Your lifestyle and being yourself is what they admire. A lot of people have not come to the realization that GOD loves them. When you can absorb this, it doesn't matter what your husband thinks or anybody else. Just "do" you.

ABOUT THE AUTHOR

The best part of Lucille's life, as she describes it, is knowing that Jesus loves her. The first question that arises the moment she hears of someone passing is, "Did they accept Jesus into their heart?" She will go right up to anyone facing death and ask that life-changing question. And she'll approach others with encouragement: "Has anyone ever told you God loves you and has a wonderful plan for your life?" She knows that God is omnipotent, and that settles it for her.

Born in Alabama, she has traveled and lived in several different states, but has now found her way back home. From her teenage years, she recalled writing love letters for close friends. Her book focuses on the lives of women coming out of challenging relationships, mainly divorces. Lucille's writing is not limited to just this type of self-help. Some of her favorite writing includes allegory and short stories. She also enjoys reaching out to women in prison, where she served as a volunteer prayer counselor.

While assisting with Bible study groups in youth centers, she aided in winning 45 young girls to Christ all, under the age of 21.

Lucille is the CEO of her elderly home business, Candlelight Compassions, in her home town. She still awaits any and every opportunity to share the Gospel and to see the lives of people changed. She also enjoys being at home again, where she was raised as a little girl. She remembers this is where it all started in a small little town surrounded by a lot of love and a lot of memories.

"I started this book in 2002 at the age of 47," says Lucille. "I'm now 58 and published. I mention this to note that it's never too late to walk in your dream, no matter what it is — as long as you give God all the glory."

Lucille Ankum would love to hear from you! Email the author at candlelight.compassions@yahoo.com. Printed and electronic versions of the book are available at Amazon.com.

www.ingramcontent.com/pod-product-compliance
Lightning Source LLC
Chambersburg PA
CBHW050348280326
41933CB00010BA/1383